Barbecuing, Grilling & Smoking

RON CLARK
BRUCE AIDELLS
CAROLE LATIMER
Writers

JILL FOX
Editor

ERNIE FRIEDLANDER
Photographer

JOANNE DEXTER
Food Stylist

JANET NUSBAUM
Photographic Stylist

A graduate in English literature from Texas A & M University, **Ron Clark** *(far left)*, writer and recipe developer of the Grilling and the Barbecuing chapters, was trained as a chef under the tutelage of Chef Wily Koln at the Royal Sonesta Hotel in New Orleans. Mr. Clark worked for many years in restaurants throughout New England and then expanded his knowledge in meat by training as a journeyman butcher. He currently manages a specialty sausage-making company. **Bruce Aidells** *(above right)*, is the writer and recipe developer of the Smoking chapter. As a restaurant chef in Berkeley, California, he gained a reputation for lively presentations and innovative dishes. He is the owner of Aidells Sausage Company, which has received national acclaim for its fine sausages and smoked meats. Mr. Aidells has collaborated on three cookbooks, including the California Culinary Academy Series' *Regional American Classics*. He has been featured in *Bon Appétit* magazine, to which he contributes articles periodically. **Carole Latimer** *(above center)*, the writer and recipe developer of the Campfire Cooking chapter, is a fifth generation Californian who has been organizing and leading wilderness adventures through her company, Call of the Wild/Outdoor Woman's School, since 1977. Her trips feature gourmet meals with fresh herbs, fruits, and vegetables from the Latimer family garden and orchard in the California Gold Country. Ms. Latimer has written articles on preparing fine food on the trail and has worked in product promotion for media tours.

The California Culinary Academy In the forefront of American institutions leading the culinary renaissance in this country, the California Culinary Academy in San Francisco has gained a reputation as one of the most outstanding professional chef training schools in the world. With a teaching staff recruited from the best restaurants of Western Europe, the Academy educates students from around the world in the preparation of classical cuisine. The recipes in this book were created in consultation with the chefs of the Academy. For information about the Academy, write the Office of the Dean, California Culinary Academy, 625 Polk Street, San Francisco, CA 94102.

Front Cover
Combine barbecued Georgia Chicken (see page 90) and Grilled Corn (see page 34) for a summertime feast.

Title Page
Creole Skewers (see page 29) put sausage, vegetables, and seafood together on the grill.

Back Cover
Upper Left: Herb Crusted Steak (see page 14) is the centerpice of this hearty meal. Grilling is a clean, quick cooking method that reserves the flavors and freshness of meat and vegetables. Grilling information and recipes begin on page 4.

Upper Right and Lower Left: Once the basic cooking techniques of grilling, smoking, barbecuing, and campfire cooking are mastered, just about every type of food can be prepared outdoors.

Lower Right: A colorful Ratatouille of Smoked Summer Vegetables (see page 63) takes advantage of the bounty of summer. Smoking recipes begin on page 44.

Contributors

Calligraphers
Keith Carlson, Chuck Wertman

Additional Photographers
Alan Copeland, pages 32, 37, 63, 68, 74, and 94
Saxon Holt, pages 11, 46, 49, 104, and 106
Kit Morris, writers and chefs, at left
Richard Tauber, page 43

Additional Stylists
Carole Latimer, pages 11, 46, 49, 104, and 106
Clay Wollard, page 43

Copy Chief
Melinda Levine

Copyeditors
Toni Murray
Andrea Y. Connolly

Proofreader
Karen K. Johnson

Indexer
Nancy Mulvany

Editorial Assistant
Tamara Mallory

Compositor
Bob Miller

Series Format Designed by
Linda Hinrichs, Carole Kramer

Production by
Studio 165

Separations by
Color Tech. Inc.

Lithographed in the U.S.A by
Webcrafters, Inc.

Acknowledgments appear on page 127.

The California Culinary Academy series is produced by the staff of Ortho Information Services.

Publisher
Robert J. Dolezal

Editorial Director
Christine Robertson

Production Director
Ernie S. Tasaki

Series Managing Editor
Sally W. Smith

Systems Manager
Katherine·L. Parker

Address all inquiries to
Ortho Information Services
P.O. Box 5047
San Ramon, CA 94583

3 4 5 6 7 8 9
89 90 91 92 93

ISBN 0-89721-145-6

Library of Congress Catalog Card
Number 87-072101

Chevron Chemical Company
6001 Bollinger Canyon Road
San Ramon, CA 94583

C O N T E N T S

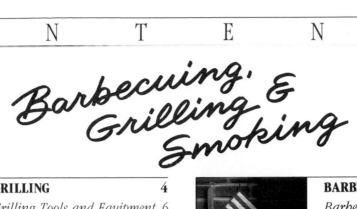

Grilled dishes in this chapter were tested on a covered, kettle-shaped grill used outdoors. Most recipes can be adapted to cooking on an open grill, either indoors or out.

Grilling

T he original cooking method—
heating food over an open flame—has
progressed to a culinary discipline
divided into distinct categories: grilling,
smoking, barbecuing, and campfire cooking.
This chapter will explore the world of
grilling, which has been popularized by recent
food trends, notably California cuisine.
Grilling is essentially a method of cooking
impeccably fresh seasonal ingredients over hot,
smoky charcoal. There are, however, many
variations on this simple theme. In this chapter
you will learn the differences between
direct- and indirect-heat cooking, the types of
charcoal available, the latest grill
technology, and many, many recipes.

Enjoy the teeming bounty of the sea by grilling clams, oysters, mussels, and lobster over a hardwood fire. New England Shellfish Roast (see page 34) is a quick, easy, and sumptuous feast. This recipe is a real crowd pleaser and is perfect for entertaining. These dishes are as good to eat as they are fun to watch during cooking: The clams, oysters, and mussels are done when the shells pop open; the lobster is done when the tail starts to curl.

TOOLS AND EQUIPMENT

The world of outdoor cooking has come a long way since the days of cooking franks and burgers over an open grill. Significant advances in the design of backyard cookers now enable you to produce exquisite meals that you never thought possible. Listed here are basic grill shapes and types and other equipment you may find useful for grilling as well as for smoking, barbecuing, and in some cases for cooking over a campfire. Recipes in this chapter were tested on a kettle-shaped grill, though you can adapt them for use on the piece of equipment you own.

Some of the other equipment such as a drip pan and an instant-read thermometer, neither of which is very expensive, are essential for more sophisticated recipes. For simpler

fare, little equipment is needed. In most cases standard kitchenware can be used, although use on and around the grill is hard on tools not designed for that use. Although you do not have to purchase a great deal of equipment to enjoy grilling, you may find it beneficial to have some of these items for your outdoor cooking.

Kettle-Shaped Grills

The kettle-shaped grill revolutionized outdoor cooking. The sophisticated design eliminated the need to control heat by lowering and raising the grill, and saved the cook from constant battles with flare-ups and uneven heat. The kettle-shaped grill is designed for cooking with the lid closed. Carefully placed vents in the top and bottom provide adequate airflow to keep the fire going and completely eliminate flare-ups. Thus, searing over a very hot fire can easily be accomplished without burning the food. If the coals are moved to each side of the kettle and a drip pan positioned in the center, food can also be cooked more slowly; this is the indirect-heat method of cooking (see page 12). Although not quite as easy to use as water smokers, kettles can also be used for slow smoke cooking (see page 78).

There are two main drawbacks to the kettle-shaped grill, however. First, the lid is not hinged, which causes some inconvenience every time you open and close it. Second, the grill position is not adjustable; if the food is not quite ready but the fire is dying out, it's not possible to move the food closer to the coals to finish the job. You are left with two options: finish under your kitchen broiler or remove the food and rebuild the fire.

Gas Grills

The most recent step forward in the high-tech world of outdoor cooking is the introduction of a new generation of gas grills with sophisticated heat circulation and control. You'll find versions with either lava rock or porcelain-coated metal bars. Both serve the same function—they evenly emanate heat from the gas burners below them and vaporize drippings from the food above, giving the food that distinct grilled flavor. In time a difference between the two versions becomes evident, however. The lava rocks are nearly impossible to clean effectively; the layers of burned grease give food an unpleasant flavor. The porcelain-coated bars are easily removable for cleaning and are dishwasher-safe.

Probably the greatest asset gas grills offer is the ability to control cooking temperatures. Most units have three horizontal gas burners, which allow you to regulate the heat to the desired temperature. By experimenting a bit, you will find the gas grill to be just as accurate and responsive as your kitchen oven.

The primary drawback of cooking on gas grills is the difficulty of imparting a distinctive smoked flavor. Hardwood chunks are too big to burn effectively, and hardwood chips tend to burn too quickly. The best way to achieve acceptable smoked flavor is to carefully replenish the chips as they burn.

The second drawback is one of personal attitude. To some, cooking on a gas grill just doesn't seem like traditional outdoor cooking. How can food cooked over a gas grill even begin to taste as good as food cooked over a mesquite grill laden with applewood chips? This is a legitimate objection, but it is primarily emotional and romantic. The truth of the matter is that a gas grill is as good as the person cooking on it. Memorable and exceptional food can be produced on a gas grill—food that is just as good or better than fare from a charcoal grill. You just have to learn how to use a gas grill to produce the desired effects.

Rectangular Hinged Grills

A number of people insist that rectangular grills are better than kettle-shaped grills. Rectangular grills do have the advantage of heat control: To attain this the grill height can be raised or lowered. You can also add briquettes, hardwood chips, or moistened fresh herbs to the fire more easily than when using a kettle-shaped grill. Also, a hinged lid makes opening and closing much easier. But when it comes to real heat control and even cooking, kettle-shaped grills are better. The rectangular grill simply cannot match the heat circulation of the kettle, and flare-ups on the grill are harder to control.

Open Grills

Recipes in this chapter were developed for use with a covered grill, but you can use them with your open grill if you improvise a lid. Try using a large cooking pot or the lid to an electric frying pan to cover the food, or make a foil tent.

Open grills are not as easy to use as kettle-shaped grills, but they are often less expensive. Since they don't have a lid, you are very likely to experience flare-ups during cooking. The best way to handle this is to use an open grill to cook only foods that don't have an oil-based marinade or foods that are low in fat, such as fish and poultry. You can't effectively use the indirect-heat method of cooking (see page 12) when using an open grill because most of the heat simply wafts into the air. Keep a spray bottle handy to control flare-ups.

Indoor Grills

Although this book was developed for cooking outdoors, most of the grilling recipes can be adapted for use on an indoor grill. The most current indoor grills can be incorporated into the stove top or set up on kitchen islands, providing a year-round grilling appliance. Both electric and gas models are available. Whatever style of indoor grill you choose, be sure it is correctly installed and that proper ventilation is maintained. Check the manufacturer's instructions for recipe adaptation methods, especially regarding cooking with marinades and the use of oil to prepare the grill.

Basting Brush

There is no need to splurge on fancy wood-handled brushes. The five-and-dime store version with a twisted-wire handle works just fine for outdoor use. Basting brushes should have long handles so that you don't burn yourself while basting.

Charcoal Rails

Designed to hold charcoal in even piles on each side of the drip pan, charcoal rails are really a bit of an extravagance. The sides of the drip pan can do just as good a job holding the charcoal in place.

Drip Pan

A drip pan is an essential for the indirect-heat method of cooking (see page 12). Your best bet is to purchase a disposable aluminum pan—a 2- to 3-inch-deep rectangle—and throw it out after each use.

Grill Brush

This inexpensive tool is a must for proper grill care. Brush grill before oiling, and after cooking, while the grill is still hot, to remove any food particles or burned-on grease. If you follow this procedure consistently, you won't have to wash the grill with cleanser, which ruins the seasoning.

Hinged Wire Basket

These baskets hold fish fillets, hamburger patties, or bread between two grills secured by a latch. Simply place the food inside the basket and place the basket over the heat. When one side is done, flip it over. It is a good idea to lightly oil the basket before placing food inside.

Instant-Read Thermometer

Old-style thermometers take too long to work to provide accurate cooking temperatures for grilled foods. The instant-read versions provide an accurate picture of the progress within five seconds of insertion.

Roast Racks

Made of aluminum or stainless steel, V-shaped roast racks do an excellent job holding large pieces of meat or poultry together as they cook. If you use one while cooking with indirect heat, you don't need to turn the meat at all; it cooks evenly on all sides.

Skewers

Metal and bamboo are common skewer materials. Metal skewers, of course, never burn up, but you do have to wash them. You need to soak bamboo skewers in water for 15 to 30 minutes before use to prevent their burning. If you are fortunate enough to have rosemary growing nearby, try using these branches for skewers. Remove the needles and soak the branches in water for 30 minutes. They imbue the skewered food with a pungent rosemary flavor.

Spatula

Take the time to find an offset stainless-steel spatula with a blade 5 to 6 inches long—the kind professional chefs use. The advantage of the long blade is that it will slide under most chops and fish fillets completely so that they won't tear or stick when being flipped over. Stainless steel will never rust and is easy to care for.

Spray Bottle

With the advent of kettles and gas grills, there aren't many fire flare-ups anymore. But always keep a spray bottle filled with water next to your grill, just in case of an emergency.

Tongs

Tongs are probably the most useful and versatile grill tool that you can buy. Use a pair that is at least 12 inches long and spring loaded. It's not a bad idea to have two pairs, one to move hot charcoal around and one to use with food. (Of course, you can get by with one pair—you will just have to keep washing it off every time you use it to move charcoal.)

FUELS

Shopping for fuel in a well-stocked market can be quite a confusing experience. Traditional charcoal briquettes are now surrounded by many different competing fuels. Mesquite charcoal; hardwood charcoals; hardwood-flavored charcoals; "self-lighting" briquettes; and a number of different types of smoke-creating hardwood chips, chunks, and sawdust all crowd the shelf. They all work well in the right situation. You must judge what will work best for you.

Charcoal Briquettes

Charcoal briquettes are made from wood chips smoldered into carbon, then bound together with fillers and starch and pressed into a uniform shape. Self-lighting briquettes are formed by the addition of petroleum products. Before beginning to cook over any briquettes, wait until they are completely coated with a thin layer of gray ash. This means that all the additives have burned off. Long, slow cooking requires that you replenish your fire with more briquettes, so you will be faced with the dilemma of how to add fresh briquettes without adding chemical fumes from the additives to your food. One solution is to start your second set of coals in a charcoal chimney—a large, vented metal can—and add them to your grill after they are covered with gray ash. A distinct advantage of charcoal briquettes is that they burn evenly and consistently. For an average fire that lasts about an hour, count out 30 to 40 briquettes. Plan on adding 16 to 20 for each additional hour.

Mesquite Charcoal

Mesquite is a scrub hardwood tree that covers the arid plains of the Southwest and Mexico. It has long been used in those areas as a fuel for outdoor cooking and is rapidly becoming the most popular outdoor-cooking fuel source across the country. Mesquite charcoal is simply mesquite that has been carbonized by slow smoldering in controlled conditions. There are no additives or fillers of any kind. The advantage of mesquite is that it burns much hotter than charcoal briquettes and most other hardwood charcoals. As a result, you don't have to use as much, and the high cooking temperature produces a much tastier product. Mesquite also provides a subtle smoky flavor that is not nearly as pronounced as that of fruitwoods, oak, or hickory. Leftover pieces of mesquite charcoal can be reused, something that can't be said for charcoal briquettes. Light mesquite as you would any other charcoal, but be particularly careful about high winds or nearby trees. Mesquite charcoal pops and crackles a lot when first lit, and can eject burning embers into the air. Extra supervision is required.

Hardwood Charcoals

Although not nearly as prevalent as mesquite charcoal, other hardwoods are carbonized in the same manner as mesquite to form excellent fuel sources. The advantage of hardwood charcoals is that they provide a flavorful smoky complement to your food; the disadvantages are scarcity, price, and—most significant—the inability to burn as hot as mesquite. Try using mesquite charcoal as your fuel source and presoaked hardwood chunks as your smoke source.

For the average fire, use between 3 and 4 pounds of either mesquite or hardwood charcoal in your grill. You may need more or less, depending on the size of the charcoal. (Sometimes during shipping the charcoal breaks up into tiny pieces, which burn quickly.) Add an additional 2 to 3 pounds of charcoal hourly to maintain the fire.

Woods

Use oak, hickory, cherry, apple, mesquite, or alder as a wood for outdoor cooking. Be aware, however, that although a wood-burning barbecue is romantic, it doesn't make much sense. Wood takes a considerable time to burn down to usable coals, and wood coals don't last as long as either charcoal briquettes or hardwood charcoal. With wood you end up waiting twice as long to cook, and then your fire goes out sooner. Instead of using these woods as your major fuel source, use the smaller pieces as kindling, and cut the remainder into 1-inch chunks to add a smoky complement to your fire. Never use a softwood for either smoking or as a fuel; the thick resins produce a distinctly unpleasant aftertaste. Be careful about burning scrap wood. Pressure-treated lumber (the type of wood used in outdoor construction), for instance, contains chemicals that can be toxic.

Hardwood Chunks and Sawdust

Food cooked over hardwood has a distinctive smoky flavor. Hickory, alder, mesquite, and applewood are the most popular and available woods.

If you use a gas grill, hardwood chips work better than chunks. Select pieces ½- to 1-inch thick and soak them in water for at least 30 minutes before you use them. Place an old aluminum pie pan over the gas heating elements toward the back corner of your grill before you turn it on, and place the water-soaked chips in the pan. As the grill heats up, the chips will begin to smolder. You may experience flare-ups from the chips if you cook with high heat, so have your spray bottle ready. The only limitation of this method is that the chips tend to burn quickly. You'll have to monitor the progress and replenish the chips as necessary, but don't put too many on at once lest you extinguish your fire.

For the gas grill, hardwood sawdust works as well or better than hardwood chips. Easy to ignite, sawdust provides a consistent, flavorful smoke. To use, place sawdust in an old pie pan and place directly on top of lava rocks or flavorizer bars. Turn gas burners to high until sawdust just blackens and begins to smolder. Immediately turn burner underneath pan off. Replenish sawdust as needed. Hardwood sawdust is available at lumber mills and specialty cookware stores.

Fresh Herbs and Citrus Rinds

Thyme, bay, rosemary, oregano, and marjoram are particularly well suited to flavoring your fire. Chose one type of herb and simply moisten it with water (use wine or liquor to moisten it for an added taste treat), and toss it onto the coals right before you put food on the grill. Try lemon, orange, or lime rinds as well. Add them one at a time, with or without a complementary fresh herb. Be careful not to directly inhale the fumes of burning herbs or fruit rinds, however—they can be rather powerful.

Please the most militant meat-and-potato fan with this classic combination of Herb-Crusted Steak (see page 14) and rosemary-accented Potato Wedges (see page 34). Roasted Garlic (see page 37) is soft, spreadable, and absolutely divine as an appetizer or side dish topping Brie cheese on sliced French bread. Round out the meal with a tossed green salad.

... FOR SAFE GRILLING

☐ Grills are designed for outdoor use only. Toxic fumes may accumulate and cause serious injury or death if used indoors.

☐ Do not use grills in high winds.

☐ Do not use gasoline, alcohol, or other highly volatile fluids to ignite charcoal. Use only a commercially prepared fire starter and make sure that any fluid that may have spilled is cleaned up before igniting the charcoal.

☐ Grill should be kept in a level position at all times.

☐ Infants, children, and pets should never be left unattended near a hot grill. Since leaving the grill for a few minutes while it is hot is inevitable, consider purchasing a portable screen to place around the grill when in use to prevent people and pets from bumping into the hot grill.

☐ If the area around your grill is a shared space, come up with some kind of sign to place on the grill to indicate that the grill is in use and should not be touched.

☐ Do not place tabletop grills on glass or combustible surfaces. Heat can be conducted through the legs of the grill.

☐ Grills should never be used within 5 feet of any combustible material.

☐ Do not wear clothing with loose, flowing sleeves while barbecuing.

☐ Lighter fluid should never be added to hot or even warm coals. After use, lighter fluid should be capped and placed a safe distance from fire.

☐ Do not add self-starting briquettes—the kind impregnated with lighter fluid—while food is cooking.

☐ Never touch the heat source or the grill to see if they're hot.

☐ In case of flare-up or sparks, keep a spray bottle filled with water next to your grill at all times.

☐ If you use a kettle-shaped grill, the lid should be removed while starting the fire. Most styles have a hook on the back of the lid so you can place the lid right on to the kettle.

☐ To prevent damage to your plants and patio area, do not place a hot lid on carpet, grass, or wood deck.

☐ Always use proper barbecue tools with long handles. Do not leave tools on the grill.

☐ Wear fireproof mitts to protect hands while cooking.

☐ Do not use fringed dish towels in place of mitts or potholders, the fringe can easily catch fire as you reach across the grill.

☐ Liquid petroleum (L.P.) gas tanks for gas grills should always be turned off when not in use.

☐ Remove ashes only after all coals have completely burned out. During cooking, the ashes may contain hot coals. Remove excess ashes and used briquettes before lighting the fire for each use.

☐ Never attempt to move a hot barbecue grill.

FIRE STARTING

Whatever method you use, allow about 30 to 45 minutes for your fire to start. Be sure to follow all the Tips for Safe Grilling. The idea is to start a fire in your grill, not in your house.

Kindling

Starting a fire with kindling is probably the most individual and ritual-laden method. Although each fire starter has a unique style, the basic method is to start with a few sheets of your favorite newspaper and crumple them loosely or twist them into "logs." Place these logs in the bottom of your grill, and then place a handful of dry kindling on top. Place five or six briquettes on top of the kindling. Light the newspaper and hope for the best. If the briquettes do not light, add more newspaper and kindling until they do. Once the briquettes light, add more briquettes on top until you have a fire of the desired size. Everyone seems to have their own ratio of newspaper to kindling to briquettes. Just do what works for you.

Electric Starter

Electricity is certainly the easiest and most foolproof means of starting a fire. Check the manufacturer's recommendations for starting a fire with an electric starter in your grill. In most cases, the instructions tell you to arrange your briquettes in a pile on top of the starter, plug it in, and let it go to work. In about 10 minutes, your briquettes should be started. Don't leave your starter in any longer, or the heating element will be damaged by lengthy exposure to high heat. The only disadvantage to this fire-starting method is that you need to be near an electrical outlet.

Charcoal Chimney

The simplicity and ease of charcoal chimneys make them a wonder to watch. A charcoal chimney is nothing more than an open-ended sheet-metal cylinder vented at the lower end, with a grate about 4 inches from the bottom to set the charcoal briquettes on. To use, simply crumple several sheets of newspaper and place them under the grate. Fill the chimney with charcoal briquettes, and place in the bottom of the grill. Open the bottom vents of grill and light the paper. In about 10 minutes the briquettes will begin to smolder. Once all the briquettes are well ignited, pour them out of the chimney into the bottom of your grill.

A charcoal chimney is also the answer when you will be using your grill for several hours and don't want to replenish your fire with "raw" charcoal briquettes because of the fumes they emit when they just start to burn. Simply set the chimney on an old pie pan on a concrete surface and light more charcoal. When the briquettes are ready, pour them onto your existing fire.

You can make your own charcoal chimney by cutting the top and bottom off a number 10 can and making a vent in the bottom with a can opener. If you buy a ready-made chimney, you will find that it is inexpensive and has the added benefits of a wooden handle and a grate to set the charcoal on.

Lighter Fluid

Follow all safety procedures listed on the can when using lighter fluid. Never squirt the fluid directly onto a burning fire. The flame can easily travel back up the stream and ignite your hands and arms, not to mention the can itself! Never use gasoline, naphtha, paint thinner, or kerosene—they are too flammable for this purpose. Use only a product specifically labeled as lighter fluid.

HOW MUCH FIRE?

When determining the size of your fire, first imagine the cooking surface that the food requires. Spread the briquettes out in a single layer to cover an area about one inch past the edges that you have imagined. Now add about half again as much charcoal, and you should have enough for an hour's worth of fire. Usually 30 to 40 briquettes are sufficient to cook food for four people. If you are making a fire for slow cooking using the indirect-heat method (see page 12), use about 25 briquettes on each side of the grill. Plan on adding 8 to 10 briquettes to each side for every hour of additional cooking time.

WHEN IS THE FIRE READY?

It usually takes between 30 and 45 minutes for a fire to be ready for cooking. Never cook over a fire until the briquettes are covered with a light ash and are no longer flaming. Cooking over a direct flame only burns the outside of your food, leaving the inside raw. Your hand is probably the best judge of when a fire is ready. Hold your hand flat over the fire at grill height. You will be able to hold your hand over a very hot fire for about 2 seconds. If the fire is hot, you can hold your hand above it for 3 to 4 seconds. If you can hold it any longer than that, you have let the fire die down too much. Add more briquettes and let it build up again. A very hot fire is ideal for the direct-heat method of cooking (see page 12); a medium to hot fire is desirable for the indirect-heat method (see page 12). Once your fire is ready, carefully add hardwood chips or fresh herbs. Put the grill in place and let it heat up for 4 to 5 minutes before putting on food.

PREPARING THE GRILL

☐ Always arrange the fire so that there are areas of the grill with no fire under them. If some of your food is done sooner than others, move it to these cooler spots to keep finished food warm while the remainder of the meal cooks.

☐ Brush the grill lightly with oil right after you put it in place over the fire. To do this, moisten a paper towel with oil. Using tongs held in a fireproof mitt–clad hand, rub the oil from the towel on to the grill. This will help prevent food from sticking to the grill and will also keep the grill seasoned.

☐ Always keep the grill clean. The best method is to quickly brush the excess food off with a grill brush immediately after you remove the food. This way the remaining fire will burn off any lingering bits, and you won't have to resort to soap and water, which would ruin the seasoning of the grill surface. If you do not have a grill brush use a crumpled wad of aluminum foil held by tongs.

☐ Have all your grill tools ready and available before you light your fire. Tongs, mitts, and spray bottle are particularly important to have at your fingertips.

☐ Have extra charcoal available. There is nothing more frustrating than discovering that your fire is dying before dinner is ready and there is no more charcoal.

OUTDOOR COOKING METHODS

With the advent of covered grills, a whole new world of barbecuing opened up. Foods can now be slowly roasted over indirect heat so that they become tender and stay moist during cooking. Whether to use indirect-heat cooking or traditional grilling over direct heat depends on the type of food to be cooked and the result desired.

Direct-Heat Method

Use the direct-heat cooking method to sear foods to seal in their natural juices and to give the characteristic grilled look. Foods that are low in fat, such as poultry and fish, and foods that don't take very long to cook are ideal choices for this method. Hamburgers, chops, vegetables, skewered items, and fish fillets all fall within this category.

If using charcoal, start your fire as described on page 10. After 30 to 45 minutes, when the coals have a light gray ash covering, spread them out one briquette deep so that you have an even cooking source. Place your grill over the coals and let it heat up for 4 to 5 minutes. If you are using presoaked hardwood chips or chunks or moistened fresh herbs, spread them out over the coals right before placing food on the grill. The wood will immediately begin to smolder. Now you are ready to cook. When using a kettle-shaped grill, keep the lid closed for the duration of cooking; regulate the heat by adjusting the upper and lower vents. The beauty of this system is the total lack of flare-ups, even though the food is cooking at a very high temperature and fat is dripping onto the coals. The fat vaporizes as it hits the coals, imparting a desirable smoky flavor to the food, but the fat doesn't have enough oxygen to ignite into an undesirable flame. Also, the heat circulation in a kettle-shaped grill is excellent, cooking the food

on top as well as on bottom. You still need to flip the food over due to the short cooking time, but it does cook faster and more evenly inside a kettle. So it is very important that the lid stay closed except when you need to baste, add coals, check the food, or turn it over. Otherwise, leave the grill alone and let it cook.

If you are using a gas grill, turn all three burners to high and close the lid. Your grill should be sufficiently hot enough to cook on in about 10 minutes. Depending on the food being cooked and the desired effect, you can leave the temperature on high while cooking or turn down one or more burners. There is a nearly immediate response to the burner temperature controls, so experiment to find the exact temperature you want.

Indirect-Heat Method

The indirect-heat method of cooking is where recent advances in grill designs yield the most spectacular results. You can now cook things on the grill that were unimaginable ten years ago. Whole prime ribs, turkeys, and chickens will cook beautifully without ever needing to be turned over. Foods traditionally braised slowly in the oven with plenty of cooking liquid, such as veal breasts and pheasant, can now be done outdoors. The reason is that the food is placed over a drip pan with no direct heat under it. All the heat circulates around the food, in much the same way as in a convection oven. Thus, you won't need to turn over a large roast, for example, because it cooks just as fast on top as it does underneath. (You probably will want to turn smaller cuts to obtain equal coloration and grill marks, however.)

Another advantage of this method is the absence of the sometimes difficult-to-handle rotisserie. It simply isn't needed anymore.

If you are using a charcoal grill, prepare your coals as described on page 10. When they are covered with a light gray ash, separate them into two piles on each side of the kettle. Place a disposable aluminum drip pan between the piles. If you are using presoaked hardwood chips or chunks or moistened fresh herbs, add them to the piles now. Put the grill in place and allow it to heat up for 4 to 5 minutes before positioning the food on the grill directly over the drip pan. If you want to sear the food first, simply place the food directly over one side of the coals until it is browned, and then move it over the drip pan. Close the lid and regulate the temperature by adjusting the upper and lower vents. Since the indirect-heat cooking method often takes several hours, you will occasionally need to add more briquettes (see page 11).

If you are using a gas grill, preheat the grill with all three burners on high. The grill should be hot in about 10 minutes. Turn off the center burner and carefully position the disposable aluminum drip pan over it. Place the oiled grill in position and turn the grill heat up for 4 to 5 minutes. Place the food directly over the drip pan. Close the lid and let it cook. Regulate the temperature by adjusting the two outer burners; leave the center burner off. For recipes calling for a temperature of 350° F to 400° F, turn the burners to medium. For recipes calling for 300° F to 325° F, turn both burners to low. If you want a smoky flavor, see page 78 for a discussion of using hardwood chips in a gas grill. If you are using moistened fresh herbs, throw them directly onto the outside porcelain bars. Remember, these grills are designed to operate most effectively when the lid is closed. Open the lid only to check on or to baste the food or to add more chips or herbs.

... OF DRY SPICE RUBS

One of the easiest and quickest ways to prepare food for grilling is to use dry spice rubs. Although there are many spice combinations available commercially, try making batches to your own taste and use them to create quick and easy grilled dinners. You can store them for up to four months in a jar in your spice rack. The concept of a dried spice rub is to imbue the meat with your own particular balance of herbs and spices that will grow stronger the longer you leave the coating on the meat. The spices explode with flavor as they cook and form a delicious crusty exterior. Use dried herb leaves in the recipes below, not ground herbs; ground spices are fine to use.

In Cajun cooking spice rubs are used to blacken meats cooked in an extremely hot cast-iron skillet. You can create the same effect on your grill by using the direct-heat cooking method (see page 12) with a very hot fire, or you can create a subtle flavor by cooking over lower heat or by using the indirect-heat cooking method (see page 12). Whatever method you choose, follow these basic techniques.

1. Make spice rub by combining all ingredients and mixing well.

2. Wash and pat dry all food before cooking. Lightly oil all external surfaces of beef, lamb, pork, and poultry. Lightly coat fish with clarified butter.

3. Massage spice rub all over external surfaces of food. Depending on the type of spice mixture, use from 1 to 2 tablespoons of rub for a pound of meat, poultry, or fish. Let stand for at least 1 hour at room temperature before cooking to allow spices to permeate flesh.

4. Grill food over fire. The spices emit rather powerful vapors when cooked at high heat, so provide plenty of ventilation, and don't stand directly downwind from grill.

SPICE RUB FOR MEAT

    1 teaspoon garlic powder
    1 teaspoon fennel seed, bruised
       or crushed in a mortar and
       pestle
    ½ teaspoon thyme
    2 teaspoons black pepper
    ½ teaspoon cayenne pepper
    1 tablespoon paprika
    ½ teaspoon oregano
    ½ teaspoon salt

Makes 3 tablespoons.

SPICE RUB FOR POULTRY

    1 teaspoon garlic powder
    2 teaspoons tarragon
    ½ teaspoon sage
    1 teaspoon marjoram
    ½ teaspoon thyme
    2 teaspoons black pepper
    ½ teaspoon cayenne pepper
    1 tablespoon paprika
    ½ teaspoon salt

Makes 3 tablespoons.

SPICE RUB FOR LAMB

Herb-Crusted Lamb Chops (see page 16) made with this spice rub are shown in the photograph above.

    1 teaspoon garlic powder
    1 teaspoon fennel seed, bruised
       or crushed in a mortar and
       pestle
    ½ teaspoon thyme
    2 teaspoons black pepper
    ½ teaspoon cayenne pepper
    1 tablespoon paprika
    1 teaspoon oregano
    2 teaspoons rosemary
    1 teaspoon basil
    ½ teaspoon salt

Makes 4 tablespoons.

SPICE RUB FOR FISH

    2 teaspoons lemon zest
    1 teaspoon garlic powder
    1 teaspoon tarragon
    1 teaspoon basil
    2 teaspoons black pepper
    ½ teaspoon cayenne pepper
    1 tablespoon paprika
    ½ teaspoon salt

Makes 4 tablespoons.

BEEF GRILL

The tenderness of a cut of beef determines the method of cooking to use. Tender cuts can be cooked directly over high heat. The internal fat marbling will keep the meat moist as the outside chars into a crisp, succulent crust. These cuts come primarily from the loin, which is divided into the tenderloin, sirloin strip, and sirloin butt. The most common cuts from the loin include New York strip steak, T-bone steak, porterhouse steak, club steak, top-sirloin steak, filet mignon, chateaubriand, tournedos, and tri-tip steak. All these cuts are tender enough to cook without a marinade, but you can use a marinade if you want to imbue extra flavor. Steak cuts from the prime rib can also be grilled over direct heat. These steaks are variously called rib eyes, delmonicos, and market steaks and are the identical cut of meat.

Other beef cuts need either a marinade to tenderize the cut for direct-heat cooking or they should be cooked over indirect heat. These cuts come from the chuck, rib, cross rib, shank, flank, or leg.

When Meat Is Done

Experience is the greatest teacher for determining when meat is adequately cooked. You can also use the hand test as described in the Special Note on page 16 as a guide to when meat is done. If you need to verify your sensibilities with a thermometer, use the following temperatures as rough guidelines:

Rare: 115° to 120° F
Medium rare: 130° to 135° F
Medium: 140° to 145° F
Medium well: 150° to 155° F
Well-done: 160° to 170° F

HERB-CRUSTED STEAK

Use this grill technique for almost any cut of meat, fish, or poultry that is tender enough for the direct-heat method of cooking (see page 12), including Blackened Red Snapper (see page 28). Top-sirloin steak is featured here, but you can easily substitute New York strip, loin, filet mignon, T-bone, porterhouse, club, tri-tip, or rib-eye steaks.

> 4 top-sirloin steaks (10 to 12 oz each)
> 2 to 3 tablespoons olive oil
> 3 tablespoons Spice Rub for Meat (see page 13)
> Oil, for grill
> 4 tablespoons unsalted butter

1. Lightly coat steaks with olive oil, then massage meat with spice rub until well coated. Cover and let rest for at least 1 hour at room temperature to allow spices to imbue meat with flavor.

2. Prepare fire for direct-heat method of cooking (see page 12). If using a gas grill, use a hardwood sawdust for a smoky flavor complement. If using charcoal, add presoaked hardwood chunks.

3. When fire is very hot, place steaks on oiled grill and cook for 3 to 5 minutes on each side (depending on thickness of steak and the degree of doneness desired). Keep the lid closed during cooking. Baste the steaks once on each side with butter. The spice rub will blacken during cooking, forming a delicious and pungent herb crust. Remove from fire and serve immediately.

Serves 4.

BOURBON BEEF TENDERLOIN

The tenderloin, also called the fillet of beef, is one of the most expensive cuts of beef, so you might want to save this dish for a special occasion. Buy a whole tenderloin, about 4½ to 5 pounds, and have the butcher remove the "silver" (the shiny connective tissue that covers the top of the tenderloin). What is left is an absolutely buttery-tender piece of meat. A charcoal or gas fire works equally well for this dish.

> 1 cup bourbon
> 1 cup brown sugar
> ⅔ cup soy sauce
> 1 bunch cilantro, roughly chopped
> ½ cup fresh lemon juice
> 1 tablespoon Worcestershire sauce
> 2 cups water
> 3 to 4 sprigs fresh thyme, chopped
> 1 beef tenderloin (4½ to 5 lb), with silver removed
> Oil, for grill

1. Prepare marinade by combining bourbon, brown sugar, soy sauce, cilantro, lemon juice, Worcestershire, the water, and thyme.

2. Be sure tenderloin is completely trimmed of any fat and connective tissue. Fold the tail end of the beef back onto itself so that the fillet is of uniform thickness. Secure with butcher's string. Pour marinade over meat, cover, and refrigerate 8 to 12 hours. Turn the fillet over several times during that time.

3. Prepare fire for direct-heat method of cooking (see page 12). When fire is ready, place meat on oiled grill, reserving marinade. Cook over high heat with lid closed, turning fillet often. Occasionally baste with marinade. Fillet is cooked rare in about 30 minutes, or when a meat thermometer registers 115° F. If you want it cooked more than rare, refer to the meat chart at left. Remove from fire and cover with foil to retain heat. Let rest for 10 minutes so that juices stay in meat. Slice against the grain and serve immediately.

Serves 8 to 10.

Fresh thyme serves as a garnish for this tasty version of Bourbon Beef Tenderloin. Serve with a little libation to horse-racing fans on Derby day.

... ON WHEN IT IS DONE

Professional chefs rarely—if ever—use a meat thermometer to test food for doneness. They touch the food with their fingertips, and when it feels right it is done. How do they do it? Years of practice and experience in handling foods develops a sophisticated sense of touch and timing. Until you develop your own touch, use a meat thermometer as one indication of doneness. But you can immediately begin to develop your own master's touch by learning the following hand test.

☐ Let one hand dangle freely, relaxing it completely. With the forefinger of your other hand, touch the meaty area between your thumb and forefinger. This is what a piece of meat cooked rare should feel like.

☐ Now make a loose fist with your hand. Touch the same place again. This is what a piece of meat cooked to medium should feel like.

☐ Now tightly clench your fist. Touch the same place again. This is what a well-done piece of meat should feel like.

This test provides a quick and easy reminder that you can fall back on time and time again. Standing by the grill and unsure if that steak is done? Just try the hand test. Works every time.

FAJITAS

Fajita means "skirt steak" in Spanish; the cut is actually the diaphragm from a steer. They are often in short supply because of the popularity of this dish. You can substitute flank steak or sirloin flap meat.

>   2 *skirt steaks (2 to 3 lb total)*
>   ½ *cup olive oil, plus oil to coat onions*
>   ½ *cup lime juice*
>   1 *tablespoon minced garlic*
>   1 *teaspoon cayenne pepper*
>   1 *bunch cilantro, stemmed and diced*
>   *Salt and pepper, to taste*
>   3 *onions*
>   *Oil, for grill*
> 12 *corn or flour tortillas*
>   1 *to 1½ cups Pico de Gallo (see page 20)*
>   1 *cup sour cream*

1. Trim steaks of any external fat. Prepare marinade by mixing the ½ cup olive oil, lime juice, garlic, cayenne, cilantro, and salt and pepper. Place steaks in earthenware or glass bowl and cover with marinade. Cover and let rest at room temperature for at least 2 hours or in the refrigerator for up to 12 hours.

2. Prepare fire for direct-heat method of cooking (see page 12). Leave peels on onions, cut in half lengthwise, and lightly coat with oil. When fire is ready, place onions flat side down on oiled grill for 5 to 6 minutes, then turn them over. Cook onions until soft (an additional 5 to 6 minutes). Remove from fire and keep warm.

3. Wipe excess marinade from steaks, reserving marinade remaining in bowl. Place meat on oiled grill directly over heat and cook for 2 to 3 minutes on each side for rare, basting with reserved marinade. Remove from fire and keep warm. Heat tortillas on grill as needed.

4. To serve, slice steaks across grain into thin strips. Place meat, grilled onions, Pico de Gallo, and sour cream on tortillas and fold. Fajitas are meant to be eaten with your hands.

Serves 6.

LAMB GRILL

Lamb is a natural for grilling because excess lamb fat, which can be quite objectionable, drips off during cooking, and the remaining fat develops a wonderful charred flavor. Rib and loin chops are the most popular cuts for grilling, and butterflied leg of lamb is the all-time classic grilled roast. The chops are tender enough as they are; the leg of lamb needs a marinade to tenderize it. If you want to buy meat for skewers, use chunks from the shoulder or leg. Be sure to marinate them for a tender and flavorful kabob.

HERB-CRUSTED LAMB CHOPS

The spicy herb coating on the lamb chops forms a delicious blackened crust that imbues the lamb with flavor while holding in the juices. Loin chops are used here, but shoulder chops can be substituted if you are on a budget. Throw dampened fresh rosemary on the coals right before you grill the meat to give it an extra punch of flavor.

>   8 *lamb loin chops (5 oz each)*
>   2 *tablespoons olive oil*
>   4 *tablespoons Spice Rub for Lamb (see page 13)*
>   *Oil, for grill*
>   4 *tablespoons unsweetened butter*

1. Lightly coat lamb chops with olive oil. Massage chops with spice rub until well coated. Cover and let rest at room temperature for at least 1 hour.

2. Prepare fire for direct-heat method of cooking (see page 12). If using a gas grill, add hardwood sawdust for a smoky flavor complement. If using charcoal, add presoaked hardwood chunks. When fire is ready, place meat on oiled grill, baste with butter, and close lid. Cook for 4 to 5 minutes, turn, baste with butter, and cook for additional 4 to 5 minutes. Spices will blacken as they form a crust. Be careful not to inhale too many of the vapors from the spices as they cook—they are quite strong. Serve immediately.

Serves 4.

BUTTERFLIED LEG OF LAMB WITH CUCUMBER-MINT SAUCE

In Middle Eastern cuisines there are two basic marinades for lamb. One uses yogurt and onions; the other uses lemon juice and onions. Either can be used on any lamb cut. This dish uses the yogurt variety with a spectacular result—a lamb leg meltingly tender with a fragrant garlic flavor.

 1 onion
 1 cup plain yogurt
 1 tablespoon minced garlic
 1 bunch cilantro, stemmed
  and diced
 ¼ cup olive oil
  Salt and pepper, to taste
 1 boneless leg of lamb (7 to
  8 lb), butterflied
  Oil, for grill

Cucumber-Mint Sauce

 1 cucumber
 1 onion
 1 teaspoon minced garlic
 ¼ cup chopped mint leaves
 1 cup plain yogurt
  Salt and pepper, to taste

1. Prepare marinade by puréeing an onion in your food processor or blender. Combine onion with yogurt, garlic, cilantro, olive oil, and salt and pepper.

2. Have a butcher bone and butterfly the leg of lamb to a uniform thickness. This is very important; otherwise, it will not cook evenly. The butcher should also trim the outside fat as closely as possible and remove all interior fat and connective tissue.

3. Rub the marinade into the meat and cover. Let rest at room temperature for at least 4 hours or refrigerate for up to 12 hours.

4. Prepare fire for indirect-heat method of cooking (see page 12). When fire is ready, wipe excess marinade from meat and reserve marinade remaining in bowl. Sear both sides of meat over direct heat on oiled grill, then place lamb, skin side down, over drip pan and close lid.

You won't need to turn the lamb over during cooking. Baste occasionally with reserved marinade. Cook until meat is rare (140° F), about 45 minutes. Remove from grill and cover with foil. Allow to rest for 10 minutes for juices to collect in meat. To serve, separate leg into separate muscles— top round, bottom round, sirloin tip, and shank—and cut across the grain. Serve with Cucumber-Mint Sauce.

Serves 8.

Cucumber-Mint Sauce Peel cucumber, quarter lengthwise, and slice thin. Peel and finely dice onion and combine with cucumber, garlic, mint, and yogurt. Adjust seasoning with salt and pepper. Serve chilled.

Makes 2 cups.

Luscious Butterflied Leg of Lamb With Cucumber-Mint Sauce is meltingly tender after marinating for only 4 hours. The short marination, quick grill time, and refined presentation make this dish an excellent choice for a Saturday evening dinner with friends.

*Grilled food can transcend
backyard dining when it is as
exquisite as these rondelles of
Elegant Veal Breast and Steamed
New Potatoes (see page 37).*

VEAL GRILL

There are two types of commercially available veal in this country. Eastern veal is the flesh of a calf that has been fed only an enriched milk formula. Western veal is produced from calves that grazed on grass, which pinkens or reddens the creamy white color of the flesh. Allowing calves to graze also toughens their muscles. Eastern veal usually costs about twice as much as western veal. For that reason and because of wider availability, western veal is recommended for use on the grill.

Veal contains no internal marbling and very little external fat. Consequently, it has very little natural flavor. It accepts the flavor of marinades or larding quite well, however, and veal is a natural for the accompaniment of a sauce at the table. Stuffings go very well with roasts or with chops. Most people prefer veal well-done, or when a meat thermometer reads 155° F to 160° F. You may find this too dry; experiment to find the degree of doneness you prefer.

Use the direct-heat method of cooking (see page 12) for cuts from the loin, rib, and some cuts from the hind leg. Most commonly used cuts are loin chops and rib chops. Use the indirect-heat method (see page 12) for all other cuts, most commonly the breast, shoulder roast, and leg roast.

ELEGANT VEAL BREAST

The veal breast is a little-known and underappreciated cut of meat. Because it is tough, it is traditionally braised (cooked with moist heat). This dish takes advantage of slow indirect heat and includes pork fat to keep the meat moist during cooking. Be sure to allow plenty of time for preparation. Remember when shopping to purchase some butcher's string for this cooking method. Most of the work can be done the day before by preparing the stuffing, rolling and tying the roast, covering, and refrigerating overnight.

3 ounces pine nuts
4 tablespoons butter
1 onion (about 8 oz), coarsely chopped
1 tablespoon minced garlic
½ bunch Italian parsley, coarsely chopped
1 bunch fresh spinach
¼ cup bread crumbs
2 teaspoons minced fresh oregano
½ pound diced pancetta (Italian bacon)
½ cup ricotta cheese
Salt and pepper, to taste
1 boneless veal breast with pocket (about 4 lb)
2 pounds pork back fat
Oil, for grill

1. In a small skillet toast pine nuts in half of the butter until golden brown. In a large skillet, sauté onion, garlic, and parsley in remaining butter until soft. Add spinach and cook until limp. In a large mixing bowl combine spinach mixture, pine nuts, bread crumbs, oregano, pancetta, ricotta, salt, and pepper. Be careful to avoid pancetta, which is raw pork, when tasting. Cover stuffing and refrigerate for 1 hour. Keep stuffing cold to lessen the spread of bacteria.

2. If possible, have a butcher make a pocket lengthwise in a boneless veal breast, or do it yourself. Place stuffing into pocket until the cavity is tightly packed. Fold the roast in half from end to end and tie securely with butcher's string. Cover the top of the roast with flattened pieces of pork back fat and secure with toothpicks. Cover and refrigerate until 2 hours before cooking. At that time, allow roast to come to room temperature.

3. Prepare fire for indirect-heat method of cooking (see page 12). When fire is ready, place presoaked hardwood chips on fire. Place breast on oiled grill over drip pan and close lid. There is no need to touch the roast during the cooking process, but maintain an even cooking temperature. Roast is done in 2 to 2½ hours (155° F on a meat thermometer). Let rest 15 minutes before slicing.

Serves 8 to 10.

COLERIDGE CHOPS

If possible, have a butcher cut thick veal loin chops about 1 inch thick and make pockets in them for stuffing. You can prepare the chops a day in advance. If you do, be sure to allow the meat to come to room temperature before cooking. Italian polenta and grilled zucchini are excellent accompaniments to this dish.

2 ounces dried shiitake mushrooms
1 ounce sun-dried tomatoes (packed in olive oil)
4 ounces frozen artichoke hearts, thawed and drained
4 ounces Jarlsberg cheese, grated
½ cup bread crumbs
2 teaspoons dried oregano
½ cup plus 2 tablespoons olive oil
8 thick-cut veal chops, with pockets
1 tablespoon minced garlic
Oil, for grill

1. Soak mushrooms and tomatoes for 1 hour in just enough tap water to cover. Drain and reserve liquid for soup stocks or combine it with marinade (add bread crumbs to compensate for liquid).

2. Prepare stuffing by mixing soaked mushrooms and tomatoes, artichokes, cheese, bread crumbs, oregano, and ½ cup of the olive oil.

3. Fill pockets of chops with stuffing so that they are evenly plump. Secure openings of pockets with toothpicks.

4. Rub chops with minced garlic and the remaining olive oil to provide an even covering.

5. Prepare fire for indirect-heat method of cooking (see page 12). When fire is ready, sear both sides of each chop over heat on oiled grill, then place over drip pan and close lid. Chops are done when moderately firm to the touch, about 6 minutes per side. Remove toothpicks and serve immediately.

Serves 4.

PORK GRILL

The pig was born to be grilled. The tender, sweet flesh accepts marinades beautifully, and the high internal fat content keeps the meat moist during cooking. Most cuts of pork can be cooked over direct heat, except for large roasts and heavily marinated cuts, which may cause flare-ups. Try not to buy frozen pork—the cell walls in the meat break down very easily during freezing, causing significant water loss and a dry piece of meat. Pork should be cooked to well-done, about 145° F, but not dried out. It can be ruined by overcooking.

SUCCULENT PORK TENDERS

This dish employs a Chinese-style marinade and a tender and lean cut of pork, the tenderloin. Available in specialty butcher shops, the tenderloin requires very little cooking and is mouth-wateringly tender.

- ½ cup soy sauce
- ¼ cup sesame oil
- ¼ cup rice wine vinegar
  Fresh ginger, 2-inch piece, sliced
- 1 bunch cilantro, minced
- 2 tablespoons minced garlic
- 2 tablespoons brown sugar
- ½ cup water
- 3 pounds pork tenderloins
  Oil, for grill

1. Prepare marinade by mixing soy sauce, sesame oil, rice wine vinegar, ginger, cilantro, garlic, sugar, and the water. Trim excess fat off pork, place pork in a bowl, and cover with marinade. Cover and let rest at least 2 hours at room temperature or up to 12 hours in the refrigerator.

2. Prepare fire for direct-heat method of cooking (see page 12). When fire is ready, remove meat from bowl, reserve excess marinade. Place tenderloins on oiled grill. Cook over hot fire, turning frequently. Baste often with reserved marinade. Tenderloins are done when lightly firm to the touch (145° F on a meat thermometer), about 5 minutes.

Serves 4.

GORGONZOLA PORK CHOPS

This recipe was created by chef Bruce Aidells, author of the chapter about smoking. If possible, have a butcher cut extrathick center-cut pork chops (about 1 inch thick) and make a pocket in them for stuffing. Use a high-quality Italian sausage made with fennel and garlic. If you can't find the sausages in your local market, see the Special Note on page 121.

- ¾ pound mild or hot Italian sausage, removed from casings
- ¼ cup pine nuts, toasted
- 2 tablespoons sun-dried tomatoes packed in olive oil, minced
- ½ pound Gorgonzola cheese
- 4 thick pork chops (10 to 12 oz each), with pockets
- 2 tablespoons olive oil
  Salt and pepper, to taste
  Oil, for grill

1. In a medium skillet on the range, sauté sausage over medium heat until just done (about 10 minutes). Drain and transfer to a medium bowl. Add pine nuts, tomatoes, and Gorgonzola and mix well. Cover and refrigerate until cold (about 30 minutes). Place stuffing into pocket of each chop and seal pockets with toothpicks.

2. Prepare fire for direct-heat method of cooking (see page 12). Rub meat with olive oil; season with salt and pepper. When fire is ready, place chops on oiled grill. Cook over hot fire until just firm to the touch (145° F on a meat thermometer), about 10 minutes per side.

Serves 4.

SOUTHWESTERN PORK CHOPS WITH PICO DE GALLO

Vast lonely mesas in the Southwest are covered with the scrubby mesquite tree. Long before trendy eateries discovered mesquite charcoal, locals did their barbecuing over mesquite logs. Serve the pork chops with warm, fresh corn tortillas and generous helpings of Pico de Gallo, a salsa perfumed with cilantro and lime.

- 8 center-cut pork chops (5 oz each)
- 2 tablespoons olive oil
- 6 tablespoons Spice Rub for Meat (see page 13)
  Oil, for grill

Pico de Gallo

- ¼ cup minced onion
- ¼ cup minced green bell pepper
- ¼ cup minced red bell pepper
- 1 teaspoon minced garlic
- 1 bunch cilantro, minced
- 1 tablespoon dried chiles, diced
- ½ cup fresh lime juice
- ½ cup white vinegar
  Salt and pepper, to taste

1. Lightly coat pork chops with olive oil. Massage chops with spice rub and let marinate at room temperature for at least 1 hour.

2. Prepare fire for direct-heat method of cooking (see page 12). A mesquite charcoal fire is recommended to give an authentic southwestern flavor. When fire is ready, place meat on oiled grill. Cook chops on each side until golden brown, about 5 minutes per side. Chops should feel firm to the touch (145° F on a meat thermometer). Serve with Pico de Gallo.

Serves 4.

Pico de Gallo Combine all ingredients in earthenware mixing bowl, and adjust seasonings with dried chiles, salt, and pepper. Flavors will meld together and grow stronger with time. This is an excellent accompaniment to many grilled meats, including Fajitas (see page 16). Tightly covered and refrigerated, this sauce will keep for 3 to 4 weeks.

Makes 1 to 1½ cups.

The sweetness of simple Grilled Corn (see page 34) provides a natural balance to spicy Southwestern Pork Chops With Pico de Gallo garnish.

POULTRY GRILL

Chicken is one of the most versatile foods for grilling. It accepts almost any marinade or sauce with beautiful results. Unless skewering the meat, try to avoid boneless cuts because they tend to dry out quickly. For most recipes use fresh fryers or broilers that weigh between 3 and 4 pounds. Birds of this size are quite tender and can easily be grilled over direct heat if split, quartered, or cut into individual pieces. If you use larger birds or want to grill a chicken whole, you will probably want to use the indirect-heat method of cooking (see page 12).

When buying chickens, insist on absolute freshness. If the birds are unpackaged in the butcher's case, look for a relatively dry skin and even color. If they are bagged at the self-service counter, avoid chickens with accumulated liquid in the bags, torn bags, or any off coloration. Your senses of touch and smell are the best judges of freshness. There should be no unpleasant odors and absolutely no stickiness when touched.

There has been a great deal of media attention given lately to bacteria in chickens. *Salmonella* bacteria, which cause food poisoning in humans and other warm-blooded animals, is—unfortunately—often found in chicken. However, with proper food preparation food poisoning can easily be prevented.

Proper handling of chicken consists of defrosting birds in the refrigerator rather than on a countertop and never leaving uncooked chicken exposed at room temperature. Always remove the innards and thoroughly wash chickens inside and out before cooking. Pat dry with paper towels or a clean kitchen towel (discard or wash towels after each use). Wash all work surfaces and utensils with hot soapy water after working with chicken. *Salmonella* can live on work surfaces and be transferred easily to raw foods—such as salad ingredients that you cut up on the wooden cutting board on which you have just cut up a chicken. Make sure all poultry dishes are completely cooked before serving.

In most cases your own judgment will tell you when a chicken is done, but you can double-check yourself by inserting an instant-read thermometer into the thickest part of the breast without touching the breastbone. A reading of 165° F indicates doneness. A fork stuck between the thigh and breast should reveal slightly pink juices.

Poultry labeled "game hen" is really a type of domestic chicken. A cross between a Plymouth hen and a Cornish rooster, a game hen weighs about 1½ pounds and though rarely found fresh, is readily available frozen. Flavor them as you would chickens, and grill them using the direct-heat method of cooking (see page 12). Commercially raised game birds are increasingly available across the country. Ask your grocer to order them if you do not find them in your local store.

Ducks are also wonderful grill subjects. The overwhelming majority of commercially raised ducks are white Pekin ducks, marketed under trade names such as Long Island Duckling, Reichardt, Maple Leaf, and Culver. Ducks freeze quite well, so if you can't find them fresh, feel confident with using frozen. Ducks weigh between 3 and 5 pounds each and should be cooked over indirect heat because of their high fat content. As with chickens, wash ducks thoroughly inside and out and pat dry with a paper towel or clean kitchen towel before cooking. Prick the skin of the bird all over with a fork to allow the fat to drip out and moisten the duck as it roasts.

LEMON CHICKEN

This dish works best with the indirect-heat method of cooking (see page 12). On an outdoor gas grill, try using mesquite chunks to provide a smoky complement to the lemon-garlic flavor of the chicken. Lemon Chicken, pictured on page 39, is an excellent dish for entertaining. Although the chicken takes about an hour and a half to cook, it requires almost no attention, giving you plenty of time to prepare the rest of the meal in your kitchen, visit with your guests, or just enjoy the day. Chicken cooked this way travels well, too. After it is cooked, cover, refrigerate, and pack with you for the first night of a camping trip (when you're too pooped to cook) or for an elegant addition to a picnic.

> 1 *plump chicken (about 4 lb)*
> 2 *lemons*
> 1 *tablespoon minced garlic*
>   *Salt and pepper, to taste*
> 2 *to 3 tablespoons olive oil*
>   *Oil, for grill*

1. Prepare fire for indirect-heat method of cooking (see page 12).

2. Wash chicken thoroughly and pat dry. Peel lemons and dice the rind. Juice both lemons.

3. To make a basting mixture, combine one half the lemon rind with garlic, salt and pepper, lemon juice, and olive oil. Coat chicken inside and out with basting mixture; reserve remainder. Stuff chicken cavity with remaining lemon rind.

4. When fire is ready, place chicken on oiled grill directly over heat to sear. Sear chicken on all sides, then place over drip pan, breast side up. Close lid. Cook for 1 to 1½ hours, basting occasionally with reserved basting mixture. Chicken is done when juices run slightly pink to clear, or when an instant-read thermometer reads about 165° F. Serve hot or cover and refrigerate and serve cold.

Serves 4.

Kids' Cooking

... AT THE GRILL

This section, and the sections on pages 75, 88, and 113, are written just for kids. You might let your parents read this, but only if they ask your permission. If you have been interested in learning to cook, grilling is a terrific introduction. There is something kind of magical and interesting about cooking over an outdoor fire. When are you old enough to cook over a grill? Each child is different. Some kids may be ready at six years old; others may be teenagers before they are ready. If you are interested in learning to cook and you are tall enough to reach the grill, ask your parents if you can start learning with these easy recipes. Whatever age you are, have your parents start the fire while you concentrate on preparing the food. Have them stay around during the whole cooking time just in case you need some help. But don't let them do the cooking. This is your chance to do something all by yourself. There is no better teacher than experience.

JOSIE'S BURGER

There are a few simple tricks to grilling hamburgers that even a lot of adults don't know. One of the most important is to flavor the meat before you cook it. Second, you should make the burger patty thick to begin with so that the outside is charred while the inside is juicy. Third, don't handle the ground beef too much. The less you handle it, the lighter and fluffier the burgers will be. Here is a basic recipe for hamburgers for three people. Serve with your favorite buns and fixings.

    1 pound ground beef
    1 teaspoon salt
    ½ teaspoon ground pepper
    2 tablespoons oil for meat
      plus oil for grill

1. In a mixing bowl combine ground beef, salt, and pepper, working quickly and gently.

2. Divide mixture evenly into thirds and gently shape into patties about 1 inch thick. Pour oil onto your hands and lightly coat outside of burgers. Now wash your hands to remove all the oil and meat.

3. Have your parents or an adult help you prepare a fire for direct-heat method of cooking (see page 12). When fire is ready, place burgers on oiled grill. Cook each side for 4 to 5 minutes for rare, 5 to 6 minutes for medium, or 8 to 9 minutes for well-done. Keep lid closed during cooking. Flip the burgers over only once. Press down burgers with a cooking spatula several times during cooking so that they cook evenly. Serve immediately on warm hamburger buns with all the fixings you desire.

Serves 3.

Cheeseburgers After you flip burgers over and flatten them a bit with your spatula, lay several thin slices of your favorite cheese on top. Cheese will melt more quickly with lid closed than with it open.

Bacon Cheeseburgers Place pieces of fully cooked bacon on top of burgers right before you add cheese.

Barbecued Burger Baste the burgers with your favorite Barbecue Sauce (see page 80) as they cook. You can spread more sauce on the burgers at the table.

MARSHMALLOW ROAST

One of Josie's favorite parts of grilling is cooking marshmallows over the coals after dinner.

Marshmallows

After you take the chicken or hamburgers off the fire, add a few briquettes, close the lid, and open the vents. There should be enough fire left after dinner to toast some marshmallows. Attach one or more marshmallows to the end of a long fork or a straightened wire coat hanger. Hold marshmallow over heat until toasted. Be careful that it doesn't drop into the ashes. This is an especially fun treat when camping. See the photograph on page 120 of toasted marshmallows and other delicious campfire desserts.

SMOLDERING CHICKEN

This recipe utilizes a dry spice rub and the indirect-heat method of cooking (see page 12) to produce a spicy-hot crust and moist, succulent flesh. Smoldering Chicken is extremely easy to prepare. Allow at least one hour before grilling for spice rub to marinate the chicken. Adjust the spices in the rub to reflect your mood and taste.

1 chicken (3 to 4 lb), cut
  into pieces
2 to 3 tablespoons olive oil
3 to 6 tablespoons Spice Rub
  for Poultry (see page 13)
2 lemons
  Oil, for grill

1. Wash chicken and pat dry. Lightly coat with olive oil. Massage chicken with spice rub until lightly coated. For a 3-pound chicken start with 3 tablespoons, for a 4-pound chicken use 4 tablespoons. If you are adventurous or really like spicy food, use 5 or 6 tablespoons.

2. Cover chicken and let rest at room temperature for at least 1 hour before grilling. Juice 1 of the lemons. Cut other lemon into wedges.

3. Prepare fire for indirect-heat method of cooking (see page 12). If using a gas grill, try using hardwood sawdust to add a smoky flavor complement. If using charcoal, use presoaked hardwood chips.

4. When fire is ready, place chicken on oiled grill and close lid. Cook for about 45 minutes, turning chicken several times and basting with lemon juice. Chicken is done when juices run slightly pink to clear, about 165° F on an instant-read thermometer. Serve immediately with lemon wedges.

Serves 3 or 4.

RASPBERRY-GLAZED GAME HENS

This recipe, pictured on page 36, was developed by chef Bruce Aidells, author of the chapter about smoking. The dish is a classic combination of game hens and a raspberry glaze with a sumptuous stuffing made with his own brand of fresh herb sausage, almonds, and Gruyère cheese. If you can't find Aidells brand sausage in your local store or through the mail-order sources on page 121, substitute a high-quality French breakfast sausage.

½ pound Pork Sausage
  with Fresh Herbs, removed
  from casings
4 tablespoons unsalted butter
4 green onions, finely chopped
½ cup almonds, toasted
  and lightly chopped
⅓ pound Gruyère cheese, grated
¾ cup bread crumbs
4 Cornish game hens (14 to
  16 oz each)
2 tablespoons olive oil
2 tablespoons raspberry-
  flavored vinegar
2 tablespoons raspberry jam
  or honey
  Oil, for grill

1. Sauté sausage in butter until just done (6 to 8 minutes). Add green onions and cook an additional minute. Drain grease and transfer mixture to a large bowl and combine with almonds, cheese, and bread crumbs. Thoroughly chill stuffing mixture.

2. Wash game hens and pat dry. When stuffing is well chilled, stuff and truss birds. In a small bowl combine olive oil, vinegar, and jam to form a glaze. Rub birds thoroughly with this mixture and reserve remaining glaze.

3. Prepare fire for indirect-heat method of cooking (see page 12). When fire is ready, place birds on oiled grill directly over heat. Cover. Baste birds several times with reserved glaze as they cook. Game hens are done when they are a brilliant mahogany color (about 45 minutes).

Serves 6.

LEMONGRASS DUCK

The secret to a delicious duck is to render as much fat as possible while cooking slowly to tenderize the meat. By using the indirect-heat cooking method (see page 12), the majority of fat cooks out while the skin crisps to a deep mahogany brown. The flesh is perfumed by the tangy sweetness of a lemongrass-ginger stuffing.

1 duck (4 to 5 lb)
2 stalks lemongrass
4 to 5 slices fresh ginger
3 green onions
½ bunch cilantro
2 teaspoons Chinese
  five-spice powder
2 teaspoons minced garlic
2 tablespoons Spice Rub
  for Poultry (see page 13)
  Oil, for grill

1. Prepare fire for indirect-heat cooking method (see page 12).

2. Wash duck and pat dry. Prepare stuffing by roughly chopping lemongrass, ginger, green onions, and cilantro. Combine with five-spice powder and stuff into duck. Close the opening with toothpicks or sew tightly with butcher's string. Prick duck all over with a fork so that fat will render during cooking.

3. Rub duck all over with minced garlic and spice rub. When fire is ready, add hardwood sawdust for smoky flavor if using gas. If using charcoal, add presoaked hardwood chips. Place duck on oiled grill over drip pan and close lid. Allow fire to cool down to about 350° F, and try to maintain that temperature for the duration of cooking time (about 1½ hours). Duck is done when skin is crisp and dark brown, or when an instant-read thermometer inserted between the thigh and the breast registers between 165° and 170° F.

4. Remove duck from grill and discard stuffing. Disjoint duck with boning knife or kitchen shears. Serve immediately.

Serves 2 or 3.

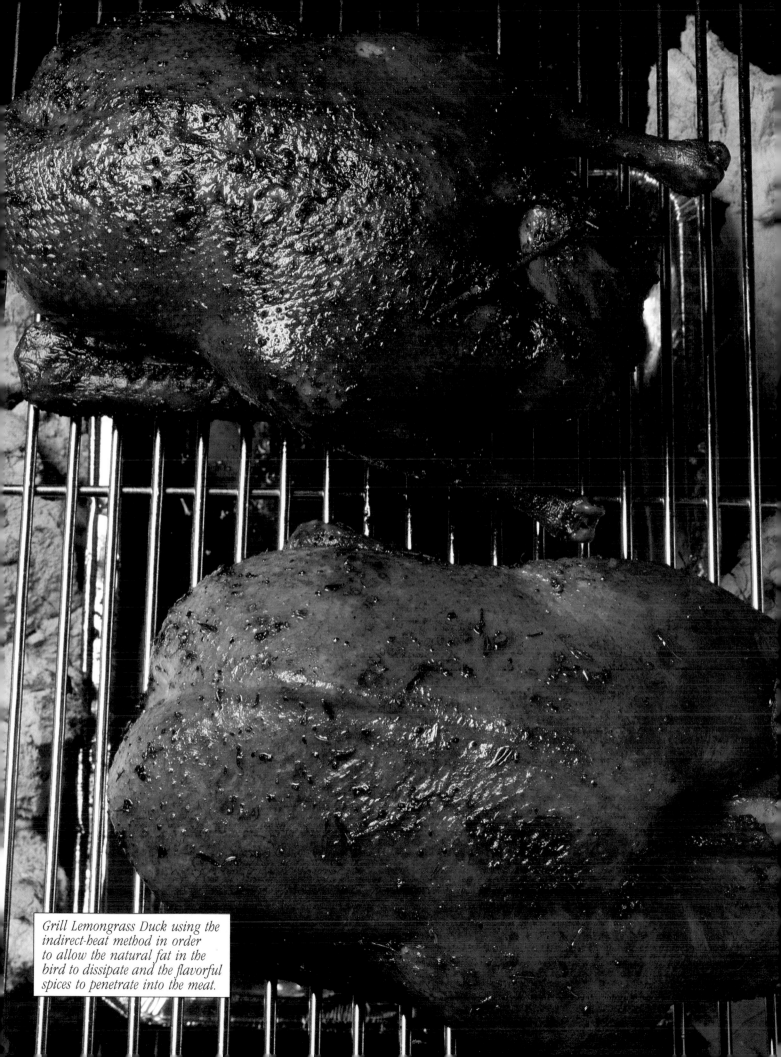

Grill Lemongrass Duck using the indirect-heat method in order to allow the natural fat in the bird to dissipate and the flavorful spices to penetrate into the meat.

TANDOORI CHICKEN

All the skin and fat are removed from the chicken before grilling, making this dish exceptionally low in calories and cholesterol. The yogurt-lemon marinade tenderizes the meat, and because it is cooked over a very hot fire, the surface of the chicken crisps up in just a few minutes, providing a delicious counterpoint to the moist and spicy flesh. Baste the chicken often with oil so that the skinless flesh won't dry out.

> 1 chicken (3 to 4 lb), cut into individual pieces
> 1 cup plain yogurt
> ½ cup fresh lemon juice
> 1 tablespoon minced garlic
> 1 teaspoon ground cumin
> 1 teaspoon ground turmeric
> ½ teaspoon ground cardamom
> 1 teaspoon ground cayenne pepper
> ½ cup chopped parsley
> Salt and pepper, to taste
> 2 tablespoons oil plus oil for grill

1. Wash chicken and pat dry. Remove skin and discard. Prepare marinade by mixing yogurt, lemon juice, garlic, cumin, turmeric, cardamom, cayenne, parsley, and salt and pepper. Coat chicken with marinade and cover. Refrigerate for at least 2 hours and not more than 6 hours. Leaving chicken in marinade overnight is not recommended; meat will become too tender and fall apart on the grill.

2. Prepare fire for direct-heat method of cooking (see page 12). Rub excess marinade from chicken and lightly coat with oil. When fire is ready, place on oiled grill meat side down and immediately close lid to avoid flare-ups.

3. Turn chicken several times while it cooks and baste frequently with oil to prevent meat from drying. Chicken will be done much quicker than you may expect due to the cooking action of the marinade and because skin is removed. Cook until golden brown (10 to 12 minutes). Serve immediately.

Serves 3 or 4.

DIVINE PHEASANT WITH SHIITAKE PÂTÉ STUFFING

Pheasant is a very rich, gamey bird that is rarely grilled since the flesh lacks oil and dries out easily. To compensate, this recipe utilizes slow cooking over indirect heat combined with a layer of pork back fat laid over the breast to continuously baste the bird as it cooks. This is a fairly sophisticated recipe, and it requires a lot of work. If you take the time, you will be rewarded with a lusciously moist, sinfully rich dinner. Pheasant are available fresh from August through midwinter.

> 2 pheasants (approximately 3 lb each)
> ½ pound pork back fat, cut into thin sheets
> Oil, for grill
> Butcher's string and toothpicks
> 1 cup duck or chicken stock
> ¼ cup crème fraîche or sour cream

Shiitake Pâté Stuffing

> 1 bunch green onions, finely chopped
> ½ cup chopped parsley
> ½ cup unsalted butter
> 1 pound chicken livers
> 1 teaspoon minced garlic
> 1 pinch each mace, cloves, nutmeg
> 2 pinches thyme
> ⅓ cup Cognac or brandy
> 4 ounces dried shiitake mushrooms, soaked in water until rehydrated, then drained
> ½ cup bread crumbs
> Salt and pepper, to taste

1. Prepare stuffing and chill. Then prepare fire for indirect-heat method of cooking (see page 12). If using a gas grill, add a hardwood sawdust; if using a charcoal grill, use presoaked hardwood chips.

2. Wash pheasants and pat dry. Stuff birds with well-chilled stuffing. Close opening with butcher's string. Tie front legs together with string. Cover top of each bird with sheets of pork back fat and secure with toothpicks.

3. When fire is ready, place birds on oiled grill directly over drip pan. Close lid and maintain a medium cooking temperature (325° to 350° F) until birds are done (1½ to 2 hours). Cooked stuffing should test about 150° F; the breast 170° F.

4. While birds are cooking, make a simple sauce by reducing stock to ⅓ cup. Right before serving, whisk crème fraîche into stock. Be careful not to boil sauce after crème fraîche is added or sauce will break.

5. To serve, remove toothpicks, back fat, and string and discard. Remove stuffing to separate serving bowl and keep hot. Split each bird in half lengthwise with large knife or kitchen shears. Lightly coat each portion with sauce. Serve one half bird to each person.

Serves 4.

Shiitake Pâté Stuffing

1. In a large skillet sauté green onions and parsley in ¼ cup of the butter until soft. Add chicken livers, garlic, mace, cloves, nutmeg, thyme, and remainder of the butter. Continue to sauté until livers are medium-rare (about 3 minutes). Remove from pan and reserve.

2. Add Cognac to pan and turn heat to high. When Cognac begins to vaporize, carefully ignite with a match. Once Cognac is ignited, gently swirl pan until fire burns out. Pour residue into liver mixture.

3. Remove any tough stems from mushrooms and slice thin. Add mushrooms and bread crumbs to liver-Cognac mixture and season with salt and pepper. Thoroughly chill. You can prepare this a day in advance and store overnight in refrigerator, but do not under any circumstances stuff pheasants until just before cooking. A stuffed bird may become a breeding ground for bacteria that could make you quite ill.

Makes 2 cups.

Note If you have never flamed liquor before, you may be startled by the result. Flames may reach 2 feet above the pan, so have a lid handy.

RABBIT GRILL

Many people say that rabbit tastes like chicken, only tougher. The statement isn't that far from the truth, but if you want to get to the core of the matter, go buy a rabbit and throw it on the grill. Rosemary is a beautiful complement to rabbit. One trendy restaurant in Northern California raised rabbits and fed them rosemary branches. The meat had a delicately perfumed essence of rosemary and didn't require any other seasoning. More than likely, your butcher shop doesn't carry rosemary-scented rabbits, but don't despair; rabbit accepts marinades well and also benefits from the tenderizing process.

DIJON RABBIT

Rabbit has often been overlooked in American cooking. This recipe will show you what you have been missing and how easy rabbit is to prepare. Although definitely chewier than chicken, rabbit is certainly worth getting your teeth into.

    1 fresh rabbit (2½ to 3 lb)
    ¼ cup unsalted butter
    3 tablespoons Dijon mustard
    1 tablespoon fresh thyme
    2 bay leaves, crushed
       Salt and pepper, to taste
       Lemon juice, for basting
       (optional)

1. Wash rabbit and pat dry. Prepare mustard coating by combining chilled butter, mustard, thyme, bay leaves, and salt and pepper. Work ingredients with your hands until the heat softens butter enough for mustard and herbs to meld with it. When soft enough to spread, coat rabbit inside and out with mustard-butter. Leave at room temperature while preparing fire.

2. Prepare fire for indirect-heat method of cooking (see page 12). If you are using a gas grill, use hardwood sawdust to create a smoky flavor. If using charcoal, add presoaked hardwood chunks, or—best of all—just use mesquite charcoal.

3. When fire is ready, place rabbit over drip pan and close lid. Do not sear first; if you do you will lose the mustard-butter coating. Rabbit will brown without searing. Turn over occasionally, spreading mustard-butter over meat as it melts. If necessary, add lemon juice or more butter or mustard if flesh looks dry. Rabbit is done when flesh is golden brown (about 45 minutes) or when internal temperature is 160° F.

4. Cut rabbit in half lengthwise down the backbone with poultry shears or large knife. Disjoint hind legs, thighs, and front legs from carcass, and then cut remaining breast and back pieces into convenient-sized serving pieces. Serve immediately.

Serves 3 or 4.

Mustard, butter, and fresh herbs sizzle and blacken as they cook on the grill and form a delicious crust for Dijon Rabbit. Poultry shears are useful for cutting the rabbit into serving-sized pieces.

SEAFOOD GRILL

Seafood is perfectly suited for cooking over direct heat. The flesh is tender because it has no tough connective tissue as red meat does. Most fish contains enough fat to stay succulent and juicy on the grill. Low in cholesterol and pleasing to the palate, fish is becoming more and more popular in American cuisine. Buy only the freshest fish available. Wash the fish in cold water to remove any bacteria and pat dry with a clean kitchen towel. You can use a marinade with fish, although usually it is unnecessary. If you do make a marinade, avoid acidic ingredients such as lemon juice or vinegar, which tend to "cook" the fish chemically. Use a very hot fire, which will seal in the natural juices. Right before putting the fish on, lightly oil the grill to prevent the food from sticking. Avoid moving the fish around on the grill, and flip it over only once—excess movement will break apart the delicate flesh.

The best test of doneness is to press the flesh with your fingertips. When fish is raw, it is relatively soft and springy; when overdone, it is hard and firm. When it is done, the flesh is "just firm." A thousand words can't describe what that means. In this case let intuition and experience guide you.

When the fish is done, serve it immediately on hot plates. There is a beauty to a freshly grilled fish, which is "alive" only for a few minutes. A famous Chinese chef in San Francisco once described his food as possessing "wok magic" for only 4 to 5 minutes after it left the wok. What he was describing is the special quality of perfectly done food when it first comes off the fire. You will ruin your dinner by keeping the fish warm while your guests meander to the table or you finish making the salad. Have everything ready, before trying your hand at "grill magic."

CAJUN SEA BASS

Sea bass has a silky-smooth, meaty texture when grilled. Imbued with the subtle smoky flavor of mesquite, this fish is an excellent counterpoint to the robust flavor of Cajun Black-Bean Sauce. If you can't find tasso in your market, try substituting a smoky-flavored bacon or Italian pancetta, and add a touch of cayenne pepper.

  6 *thick fillets sea bass,*
     (8 oz each)
  3 *cloves garlic, minced*
  ¼ *cup peanut oil*
     Oil, for grill

Cajun Black-Bean Sauce

  6 *cloves garlic, minced*
  1 *bunch green onions, sliced*
  ¼ *cup peanut oil*
  4 *ounces dried shiitake*
     mushrooms, rehydrated,
     drained and sliced
  1 *bunch cilantro, diced*
  5 *slices fresh ginger*
  4 *ounces tasso, diced*
  4 *ounces fermented black beans,*
     soaked and rinsed
  ½ *cup Shaoxing or dry sherry*
  ⅓ *cup rice wine vinegar*
  1 *cup chicken stock*
  1 *tablespoon cornstarch*
  ¼ *cup cold water*

1. Prepare fire for direct-heat method of cooking (see page 12).

2. Wash fish and pat dry. Rub fish with garlic and oil, cover, and let rest at room temperature until time to begin cooking.

3. When Cajun Black-Bean Sauce is done and fire is ready, place fillets on oiled grill. Cook until fish is just done (3 to 4 minutes per side). Remove to warm serving platter and smother with sauce.

Serves 6.

Cajun Black-Bean Sauce

1. In a large skillet on the stove, sauté garlic and green onions in peanut oil until soft. Add drained mushrooms, cilantro, ginger, tasso, and black beans. Sauté until flavors meld together (about 5 minutes).

2. Add Shaoxing, vinegar, and chicken stock to mixture. Reduce heat and simmer for 30 minutes.

3. In a small bowl mix cornstarch with the water and stir into vinegar-bean mixture. Simmer for 10 minutes more. Serve sauce over fillets.

Makes 2 cups.

BLACKENED RED SNAPPER

The popularity of blacked redfish has seriously depleted the redfish population of the Gulf of Mexico. Although redfish is flavorful, red snapper is a noble substitute, as is sea bass, sea trout, striped bass, or grouper.

  2 *tablespoons butter*
  4 *fillets red snapper (about*
     6 oz each)
  4 *tablespoons Spice Rub for*
     Fish (see page 13)
  2 *lemons*
     Oil, for grill

1. Clarify butter by melting it in a small saucepan over low heat on stove. Carefully skim as much whey (milky substance) off top of butter as possible. Tilt pan and spoon out butter, being careful to leave remaining whey on bottom of pan.

2. Wash fish and pat dry. Lightly coat fish with clarified butter. Rub fillets with spice rub. Cover fish and let rest for 1 hour at room temperature to allow spices to permeate flesh.

3. Prepare fire for direct-heat method of cooking (see page 12). Juice 1 lemon. Cut the other into wedges.

4. When fire is ready, place fish on oiled grill, skin side down. Cook until spices just begin to blacken (3 to 5 minutes). Turn and moisten blackened side with lemon juice. Cook other side until just blackened (3 to 5 minutes). Serve with lemon wedges.

Serves 4.

CREOLE SKEWERS WITH MUSTARD BUTTER

This recipe was developed by chef Bruce Aidells, writer of the chapter about smoking (see page 44). Use this simple skewer as an hors d'oeuvre or main course. For a main course serve four or five skewers per person. The spicy mustard butter is also excellent on grilled fish, chicken, or meat. It freezes well, so you can keep some on hand for last-minute inspirations or drop-in guests.

> 25 wooden skewers, presoaked in water
> 1 red bell pepper, cut into 1-inch chunks
> 1 red onion, cut into 1-inch chunks
> 1 pound Andouille sausage, cut into ½-inch-thick rounds
> 1 green bell pepper, cut into 1-inch chunks
> 1 pound large shrimp with tails, peeled and deveined
> Oil, for grill

Mustard Butter

> 1 cup unsalted butter
> 2 tablespoons minced garlic
> 3 tablespoons Creole mustard or other coarse-grained mustard
> 2 teaspoons Worcestershire sauce
> 1 teaspoon hot pepper sauce
> ⅓ cup lemon juice
> Salt and pepper, to taste

1. Skewer ingredients in the following order: red pepper, onion, sausage (push skewer through casing side of sausage so the cut edge is parallel with the skewer), onion, green pepper, shrimp (push skewer through the length of the shrimp), red pepper, onion, sausage, onion, and green pepper.

2. Prepare fire for direct-heat method of cooking (see page 12). When fire is ready, brush skewered items generously with Mustard Butter, place on oiled grill over heat, and cook for 2 to 3 minutes per side. Serve with remaining Mustard Butter.

Serves 5 or 6 as a main course.

Mustard Butter In a small saucepan melt butter. Add garlic and whisk in mustard, Worcestershire, hot-pepper sauce, and lemon juice. Season with salt and pepper. Butter can be used at this point or chilled and remelted later.

Makes 2 cups.

Succulent, grilled shrimp and spicy andouille are a classic combination in southern cooking. Combined here on a bed of rice with red onions and green and red bell peppers, Creole Skewers provide an interesting dish for entertaining. Versatile Mustard Butter freezes well so make extra and use it on other grilled fish and shellfish.

Handsome, sumptuous Grilled
Swordfish will bring to mind
romantic evenings spent on
vacation in Hawaii. Use Cilantro
Butter on bread and fish.

GRILLED SWORDFISH WITH CILANTRO BUTTER

The beauty of grilling is rarely more evident than when cooking impeccably fresh swordfish over hot smoky mesquite charcoal. (It is very important to buy fillets of uniform thickness so that they will cook evenly.) Don't do anything to the fish other than wash and lightly coat it with olive oil. Just let your own intuition and sense of timing tell you when the fish is perfectly done. Serve on hot plates with a dollop of cilantro butter. Pommes frites, a fresh salad, and hot crusty French bread would round out the meal.

> 4 center-cut fillets fresh swordfish (8 oz each)
> 2 tablespoons olive oil
>   Oil, for grill

Cilantro Butter

> 1 bunch cilantro
> ½ cup unsalted butter
>   Juice of 1 lemon
>   Salt and pepper, to taste

1. Prepare fire for direct-heat method of cooking (see page 12). Swordfish is especially good cooked over mesquite charcoal, although other types of fuel are fine.

2. Wash fish and pat dry. Lightly coat fillets with olive oil.

3. When fire is ready, place fish on oiled grill and cook until done to the touch (about 4 minutes per side for thick fillets, less for thinner fillets). Remember, in grilling fish your sensibilities are more important than exact cooking time. Serve immediately with Cilantro Butter.

Serves 4.

Cilantro Butter Wash cilantro thoroughly and remove thick stems. Combine with butter in food processor or blender and mix for several seconds with metal blade until light and fluffy. Blend in lemon juice. Add salt and pepper to taste.

Makes ⅔ cup.

MONKFISH AND WILD-MUSHROOM SKEWERS

Monkfish, also known as angler or uglyfish, is a meaty fish with a texture similar to that of lobster. It has little intrinsic flavor, so it is best prepared with a sauce or marinade. Here the woodsy flavor of fresh shiitake mushrooms combines with a classic beurre blanc to provide a delightfully light and easy meal.

> 2 red bell peppers
> 1 bunch green onions
> ½ pound fresh shiitake mushrooms
> 2 pounds monkfish fillets
> 12 wooden skewers, presoaked in water
> ¼ cup oil for coating skewers plus oil for grill
>   Juice of 1 lemon

Beurre Blanc Sauce

> ¼ cup minced shallots
> ¼ cup dry white wine
> ¼ cup lemon juice
> 1 cup unsalted butter
>   Salt and pepper, to taste

1. Stem and seed peppers, tear into 2-inch pieces, and blanch in boiling salted water until just tender. Rinse under cold water, drain, and reserve. Trim half of green stems off green onions and discard (or save for stock). Cut remaining green onions into thirds and reserve.

2. Clean mushrooms by rubbing with a damp cloth. Wash fish and pat dry. Cut fish into 1-inch cubes.

3. Prepare skewers by alternating pieces of pepper, green onion, mushrooms, and fish. Skewers are best secured by placing a piece of pepper on each end. Lightly coat food with oil.

4. Prepare fire for direct-heat method of cooking (see page 12). When fire is ready, place skewers on oiled grill over heat. Turn skewers often as they cook, and moisten fish with lemon juice. Skewers are done in 4 to 5 minutes. Serve immediately with Beurre Blanc Sauce.

Serves 4.

Beurre Blanc Sauce In a saucepan over medium heat, combine shallots, wine, and lemon juice. Cook until thick and syrupy. As sauce begins to thicken, turn heat to low, stirring often. Be careful not to burn shallots. Cut butter into ½-inch-thick pats and whisk into sauce. The secret of beurre blanc is to carefully and slowly whisk in the butter; do not allow it to boil, or it will "break," or separate. Add salt and pepper and keep warm.

Makes 1 cup.

GRILLED LOBSTER

For special occasions treat yourself to fresh lobster grilled to perfection.

> 4 live Maine lobsters (1½ lb each)
> ½ cup olive oil
> 1 tablespoon minced garlic
>   Salt and pepper, to taste
> ½ cup unsalted butter
>   Juice of 1 lemon
>   Handful fresh herbs, such as rosemary or thyme, soaked in water
>   Oil, for grill

1. Prepare fire for direct-heat method of cooking (see page 12).

2. To prepare lobster, insert knife between head and body to sever spinal cord. Cut lengthwise down the underside almost to the shell. Flatten lobster and remove the stomach, black vein, roe, and green matter (called tomalley). Wash lobsters and pat dry. Crack claws.

3. Prepare marinade in a small bowl by combining olive oil, garlic, salt, and pepper. Brush lobster with marinade.

4. In a small saucepan melt butter. Add lemon juice and keep warm.

5. When fire is ready, throw moistened herbs on fire. Place lobsters, meat side down, on oiled grill. Cook until flesh tightens and tails begin to curl (6 to 8 minutes). Turn over and cook until shells darken. Serve with lemon butter.

Serves 4.

GARLIC BLUEFISH

To New Englanders the only thing as tasty as a clambake is a freshly caught bluefish, filleted, smothered with minced garlic and olive oil, and grilled over an outdoor fire on a hot summer evening at the beach. If you live in Kansas, take heart. Thanks to overnight air shipments of east coast seafood, many people across the country now enjoy freshly caught eastern fish. As far as the beach goes, just close your eyes as you dip your feet into your pool and pretend. There is no need to oil the grill before cooking bluefish. The natural oils in the fish will take care of it for you.

> 1 tablespoon minced garlic
> 2 tablespoons olive oil
>   Salt and pepper, to taste
> 2 large bluefish fillets
>   (approximately 1 lb each)
>   Handful fresh herbs, such
>   as thyme, rosemary, or
>   oregano
>   Juice of 1 fresh lemon
> 1 lemon, cut into wedges

1. Rub garlic, olive oil, and salt and pepper into bluefish and let rest for 30 minutes at room temperature.

2. Prepare fire for direct-heat method of cooking (see page 12). If using a gas grill, use hardwood sawdust to create a smoky flavor complement. If using charcoal—which is highly preferable in this case—use presoaked hardwood chips. When fire is ready, throw moistened herbs on coals. Place bluefish, meat side down, on grill and close lid. Bluefish is a very oily fish and will take longer to cook than others. Cook 6 to 8 minutes per side, moistening flesh with lemon juice as it cooks. Serve immediately with lemon wedges.

Serves 3 or 4.

HOT AND SPICY THAI SQUID SKEWERS

Squid skewers are an unusual yet extremely easy dish to prepare. You can personalize it by adjusting the amount of hot chile oil, sesame oil, and dark soy sauce. A marinade should be stronger than the desired taste of the finished dish, but be very careful with the soy sauce and hot chile oil. Diners can always add more heat at the table, but it's difficult to take it away.

> 2 pounds squid
> 1 teaspoon minced garlic
> 1 teaspoon minced ginger
> 3 tablespoons minced cilantro
> ¼ cup peanut oil
>   Hot chile oil, to taste
>   Sesame oil, to taste
>   Dark soy sauce, to taste
> 8 wooden skewers, presoaked
>   in water
> ½ cup Thai Dipping Sauce
>   (see page 86)
>   Oil, for grill

1. Clean squid thoroughly, cutting bodies into ¾-inch strips. Pat dry.

2. Prepare marinade by mixing garlic, ginger, cilantro, peanut oil, chile oil, sesame oil, and dark soy sauce.

3. Place squid in marinade for at least 1 hour at room temperature or 3 to 4 hours in the refrigerator.

4. Prepare fire for direct-heat method of cooking (see page 12). When fire is ready, skewer squid and place on oiled grill over a very hot fire until lightly browned (about 1 minute per side). Serve immediately with Thai Dipping Sauce.

Serves 2.

SALT-AND-PEPPER PRAWNS

This Chinese dish is utterly simple to prepare. Grill prawns over a very hot fire for a short time so that the succulent juiciness is sealed inside the salt-and-pepper casings.

> 2 pounds large prawns
>   (20 to 30 shellfish)
> 1 tablespoon peanut oil
> 2 tablespoons coarsely
>   ground salt
> 2 tablespoons ground pepper
>   Oil, for grill
> 1 tablespoon sesame oil
> 1 tablespoon rice wine vinegar

1. Prepare fire for direct-heat method of cooking (see page 12).

2. Wash prawns and pat dry. Leave them in the shells. Lightly oil prawns with peanut oil and lightly coat with salt and pepper.

3. When fire is ready, place prawns on oiled grill over hot fire and grill until light golden brown (2 to 3 minutes per side). Remove from fire and drizzle lightly with sesame oil and rice wine vinegar. Serve immediately.

Serves 4.

Japanese lacquerware is just the right showpiece for Salt-and-Pepper Prawns, served here with steamed rice. The adventurous may eat the prawns shell and all.

NEW ENGLAND SHELLFISH ROAST

An interesting variation on a Cape Cod clambake, this recipe pulls out all the stops for a grand shellfish feast. Most of the work can be done prior to mealtime, making this dish ideal for entertaining.

2 live Maine lobsters
  (1½ lb each)
2 dozen cherrystone clams
1 dozen oysters
3 pounds mussels
⅓ pound unsalted butter
  Juice of 1 lemon
  Salt and pepper, to taste
1 handful fresh thyme or
  fresh herb of choice
  Oil, for grill

1. Prepare lobsters as described in step 2 of Grilled Lobster, page 31.

2. Wash and scrub clams, oysters, and mussels. Remove beards from mussels.

3. In a small saucepan melt butter. Stir in lemon juice. Add salt and pepper to taste and keep warm.

4. Prepare fire for direct-heat method of cooking (see page 12). When fire is ready, moisten thyme with water and toss on fire. Place all shellfish on oiled grill at once. Shellfish are done when the shells open (3 to 5 minutes). Remove carefully from fire to save juices that are in the shells.

5. Drain shell juices into saucepan. Place pan of lemon butter, pan of shellfish juice, and cooked shellfish on warming rack of grill until lobsters are done. Turn lobsters when flesh is slightly soft to the touch (6 to 8 minutes). Cook on other side an additional 2 minutes. Serve with hot juices and lemon butter.

Serves 4 to 6.

VEGETABLE GRILL

Don't overlook vegetables when cooking on the grill. The simplest way to enjoy grilled vegetables is to cook them right along with a steak or chops. Slice zucchini and eggplant lengthwise ½ inch thick and rub them down with minced garlic and olive oil and sprinkle them with fresh herbs. Place them on an oiled grill over direct heat.

When grilling vegetables as a side dish rather than as a main course, it is important to develop a sense of timing. Cooking three different things on the grill so that they are all done at the same time takes practice. Start by grilling one kind of vegetable by itself until you become comfortable. Time yourself so that you will know when to put the vegetable on the fire in conjunction with your main dish. Plan on using bigger fires since multiple dishes take up more grill space.

If you are adding vegetables to meat, poultry, or seafood on skewers, cut the vegetables so that they will cook in the same amount of time as the meat or fish. An example is shrimp. You know that shrimp will cook quickly, so choose vegetables that will also cook quickly. Green onions, mushrooms, and cherry tomatoes all cook as quickly as shrimp. If you want to add green bell peppers, onions, zucchini, or other squashes, blanch them first to make up the difference in cooking time. Likewise, if you are using a meat that takes longer to cook, choose your vegetables accordingly. For 1-inch cubes of beef, try using raw pieces of red bell pepper, onion, or zucchini. Whatever kind of vegetable you use, always lightly coat it with oil so that it will cook evenly.

GRILLED CORN

This is a fun dish to make and very festive in presentation.

6 ears sweet corn, in husks
  Oil, for grill

1. Carefully peel husks away from corn but do not remove. Remove silk. Wash corn and husks.

2. Close husk around each ear and tie at the top with butcher's string. Place ears in large container of cold water to soak for at least 20 minutes.

3. Prepare fire for indirect-heat method of cooking (see page 12).

4. When fire is ready, squeeze out excess water from ears, and lay them on oiled grill. Corn cooks by steaming inside husks. Turn ears occasionally. Corn is done when husks are evenly browned (15 to 20 minutes).

Serves 4 to 6.

POTATO WEDGES

This dish is best prepared over a gas grill. The potatoes can be prepared ahead of time, and then reheated in the grill or in your kitchen oven.

4 pounds red potatoes
¼ cup olive oil, plus more as
  needed
2 tablespoons minced garlic
2 tablespoons fresh rosemary
  Salt and pepper, to taste

1. Preheat gas grill to high. In a large vegetable steamer, bring 1 inch of water to a boil. Meanwhile, cut potatoes into ¾-inch-thick wedges. Place potatoes in steamer, cover and cook until potatoes yield slightly to a fork (about 10 minutes). Cool potatoes under running water.

2. Coat potatoes with olive oil, garlic, rosemary, salt, and pepper. Place potatoes on grill and immediately turn burners to low. Close lid and cook until tender (about 45 minutes). Turn potatoes several times during cooking. Baste if necessary with olive oil. Potatoes will be a golden brown with a tender, moist interior.

Serves 6.

VEGETABLE MIXED GRILL

Lightly rubbed with olive oil and garlic and perfumed with smoke, vegetables work equally well as a main course or as a complement to a grilled meat, fish, or chicken dinner. If fresh herbs are available, try adding them to the garlic rub. Serve with plenty of fresh aioli at the table.

 1 medium eggplant (about 1 lb)
 1 pound zucchini
 1 pound yellow pattypan squash
 2 red bell peppers
 1 bunch green onions
 ½ cup olive oil
 2 tablespoons minced garlic
   Salt and pepper, to taste
 1 lemon (optional)

Aioli Sauce

 6 cloves garlic, minced
 1 egg yolk
 1 cup olive oil
 1 teaspoon tepid water
   Juice of ½ lemon
   Salt and pepper, to taste

1. Wash all vegetables and pat dry, leaving stems on eggplant, zucchini, and pattypan squash. Cut eggplant lengthwise into 1-inch-thick slices. Cut zucchini lengthwise into 1-inch-thick steaks. Quarter pattypan squash. Stem and seed peppers and cut into quarters lengthwise. Remove roots from green onions.

2. On a baking sheet mix oil, garlic, and salt and pepper. Rub all surfaces of vegetables with oil mixture. Be sure surfaces of eggplant and squashes are well covered.

3. Prepare fire for direct-heat method of cooking (see page 12). If using a gas grill, use presoaked hardwood chips for a smoky flavor complement. If using charcoal, use presoaked hardwood chunks. When fire is ready, place all vegetables on grill. Quick hands and a pair of tongs are important because the oil covering will cause flare-ups; close the lid as soon as possible. Be sure to lay vegetables crossways to grill so they don't fall into the briquettes.

4. After 5 to 6 minutes, flip vegetables over with a spatula. Moisten with extra oil if surfaces appear to be drying out rather than cooking. (Eggplant is particularly susceptible to this problem.) Close lid. Vegetables should be done in another 5 to 6 minutes. Add a squeeze of lemon juice on vegetables as they are cooking. Serve immediately with Aioli Sauce.

Serves 3 or 4.

Aioli Sauce Aioli is a garlicky homemade mayonnaise. You may want to double the recipe and use it instead of storebought mayonnaise for sandwiches such as the Dagwood Sandwich on page 75. In a small mixing bowl combine garlic and egg yolk. Slowly dribble olive oil into bowl and whisk in. Mixture will begin to build up into a thick cream. Add the tepid water and part of lemon juice as sauce becomes too thick. Continue to add olive oil, then remainder of lemon juice. Season to taste with salt and pepper. Serve at room temperature or chill if desired.

Makes 1 cup.

The bounty of summer produce provides a melange of colors and flavors for Vegetable Mixed Grill. Serve as an entrée or as a side dish paired with grilled meats or fish with Aioli Sauce, here garnished with fresh herbs.

35

The sweet, crisp skin of *Raspberry-Glazed Game Hens* (see page 24) is a perfect counterpoint to the cheesy, smooth texture of grilled polenta.

POLENTA SQUARES

If you are a fan of polenta, you may sometimes have the problem of what to do with your leftovers. This dish is so good that you may find yourself making polenta just so you can use "leftovers" to make this dish. Try substituting grits for polenta for your southern barbecues. Serve grilled polenta with an Italian mixed grill of sausages, poussins, eggplant, red peppers, and zucchini with plenty of aioli and hot crusty French bread.

> 4 cups water
> 2 teaspoons salt
> 1 cup polenta
> 6 tablespoons unsalted butter
> ½ cup grated Parmesan cheese
> ¼ cup olive oil
> Oil, for grill

1. In a large pot on the stove, bring the water and salt to a boil. Add polenta and stir constantly with a whisk until polenta begins to thicken. Transfer to a double boiler and slowly cook for 20 to 30 minutes, stirring occasionally, until thick and creamy. Whisk in butter and Parmesan. Remove from heat and pour onto a 10- by 14-inch baking sheet, spreading polenta evenly with spatula until about 1 inch thick. Chill well in refrigerator, 1 to 2 hours. If you are in a rush, quick-chill in the freezer (about 30 minutes).

2. Prepare fire for direct-heat method of cooking (see page 12). Cut polenta into 2- to 3-inch squares. Gently unmold from pan and lightly coat both sides with olive oil. When fire is ready, place squares on oiled grill and close lid. Flip over when one side is golden brown (about 5 minutes). Remove from fire when other side is golden brown (about 5 minutes more). Serve immediately.

Serves 6.

STEAMED NEW POTATOES

Any vegetable can be grill-steamed. They are particularly good as a side dish when you are slow-cooking a roast using the indirect-heat method (see page 12). When you substitute another vegetable or combination of vegetables, experiment with the length of cooking time.

> 4 pounds new potatoes
> ¼ cup olive oil
> Salt and pepper, to taste
> 3 sprigs fresh rosemary, stemmed
> 1 tablespoon minced garlic
> 6 tablespoons unsalted butter
> Oil, for grill

1. Wash potatoes and pat dry. Coat with olive oil, salt and pepper, rosemary, and garlic. Enclose in heavy-duty aluminum foil with pats of butter, carefully sealing edges of foil so that steam stays in packet. The potatoes will actually steam in their own juices.

2. Prepare fire for indirect-heat method of cooking (see page 12). When fire is ready (or main course has about 1 hour left to cook), place foil package on oiled grill in a spot not directly over the coals. Close lid. Potatoes are done when a fork passes easily through them (about 40 minutes).

Serves 4 to 6.

ROASTED GARLIC

When garlic is slowly roasted, the cloves steam inside their skins until creamy soft and deliciously sweet. Serve as an appetizer, squeezing the clove paste out of the skin and spreading over slices of French bread drizzled with the garlic juices. Brie cheese is an excellent complement. You might want to make this dish in conjunction with a slow-cooking roast because both require the indirect-heat method of cooking (see page 12).

> 6 medium heads garlic
> ¼ cup olive oil
> 4 tablespoons unsalted butter
> 4 sprigs fresh oregano
> 1 baguette French bread

1. Prepare fire for indirect-heat method of cooking (see page 12).

2. Cut the top end off the garlic heads, exposing the individual garlic cloves in their skins. Place the heads in one piece of heavy-duty aluminum foil and drizzle with olive oil. Dot with butter and lay oregano on top. Tightly seal aluminum foil to form a packet. Place on grill in a spot not directly over the coals.

3. After about 45 minutes, open packet (be careful of escaping steam) and baste heads with butter-oil mixture from bottom of packet. Reseal and continue to cook until garlic is spreadably soft (about 45 minutes more). Remove packet from grill and open carefully. Slice baguette into rounds, drizzle with butter-oil mixture from bottom of packet, squeeze softened garlic out of skins, and spread onto bread.

Serves 4 to 6.

GRILLED TOFU

This recipe was developed by California chef Chris Rishell. Try making it in conjunction with other vegetables for a Vegetable Mixed Grill (see page 35). The crucial step in preparing this dish is properly pressing the water out of the tofu. Once that is done, treat tofu like a delicate whitefish when grilling, so that it doesn't break up. Your care will be worthwhile.

> 2 pounds firm tofu
> 2 tablespoons minced
>   fresh ginger
> 2 teaspoons minced garlic
> 1 bunch cilantro, stemmed
>   and diced
> ¼ cup rice wine vinegar
> ¼ cup soy sauce
> 3 tablespoons sesame oil
>   Oil, for grill

1. Drain water from tofu package and place tofu in glass or earthenware bowl. Cover tofu with plastic wrap or waxed paper and place a heavy weight on top (such as a cast-iron skillet or a brick). Occasionally drain off water pressed out of tofu. This process should take 1½ to 2 hours. Remove weight and covering, drain off excess water, and pat tofu dry. Return tofu to bowl.

2. Prepare marinade in a medium bowl by combining ginger, garlic, cilantro, vinegar, soy sauce, and sesame oil. Pour marinade over tofu. Cover and let rest at room temperature for at least 2 hours, or preferably for 8 to 12 hours in refrigerator. Turn tofu over several times as it marinates.

3. Prepare fire for direct-heat method of cooking (see page 12). When fire is ready, remove tofu from bowl and reserve marinade. Carefully place tofu on oiled grill and close lid. Gently flip tofu over when golden brown on one side, about 4 minutes. Baste with reserved marinade. Remove from heat when second side is golden brown, about 3 more minutes. Total cooking time is 5 to 8 minutes. Serve immediately.

Serves 4.

GRILLED JAPANESE EGGPLANT

Japanese eggplant is ideal for grilling because it is thin and can be grilled whole without cutting into pieces. The outside skin browns beautifully while the sweet meat inside steams from the juices. Cooking it in conjunction with other dishes calls for timing that comes only from experience. Over a hot fire Japanese eggplant usually takes about 5 minutes to cook. If it cooks before your other dishes are done, just keep it warm by covering with foil and placing on the lid or in a cooler corner of the grill. It can be rewarmed if necessary.

> 6 Japanese eggplant (about
>   2 lb total)
> 2 tablespoons olive oil
> 1 teaspoon minced garlic
>   Salt and pepper, to taste

1. Wash eggplant and pat dry. Lightly coat with olive oil, garlic, and salt and pepper. Prepare fire for direct-heat method of cooking (see page 12).

2. When fire is ready, place eggplant over direct heat and close lid. Turn several times during cooking. Eggplant should be done in about 5 minutes.

Serves 4 to 6.

ROASTED RED PEPPERS

The sweet, intense flavor of roasted red peppers adds piquancy to numerous salads, sauces, compound butters, stuffings, and other grilled vegetables (see Andouille Stuffed Chicken Roll, page 42). Prepare this recipe on a grill, a gas range, or in an extremely hot oven (see step 2, below).

> 4 red bell peppers
> 2 tablespoons olive oil
>   Oil, for grill

1. Carefully cut away stems and wash red bell peppers. Peppers must be kept whole, so be careful not to split them. Remove seeds. Pat dry and coat the outsides with olive oil.

2. *To prepare on the grill:* Prepare fire. This is the only dish in the chapter that is cooked over a direct flame. The idea is to char the skin of the peppers so that they can be easily peeled. Be sure to wear oven mitts and use long tongs during this process. Place peppers on oiled grill over direct flame, turning often to lightly char the outside uniformly (don't burn them, char them).

To prepare on a gas range: Turn stovetop burner to high and place pepper directly on burner, turning pepper often with long tongs. Once you get the hang of this, you can use several burners at once. Be extremely careful of the open flames when you reach over to the back burners.

To prepare in an oven: Preheat oven to 500° F. Place peppers stem-end down on a baking sheet. Roast in extremely hot oven (turn on exhaust fan) until uniformly charred (8 to 10 minutes). Professional chefs use this method to roast a lot of peppers at once.

3. When peppers are uniformly charred, (it takes 3 to 5 minutes, depending on the intensity of the fire), immediately remove from heat and place in a heavy-duty paper bag, close tightly, and let rest for 10 minutes. The peppers will continue to cook inside the bag, as the flesh steams from the heat.

4. Open bag and empty peppers onto cutting surface. Let cool slightly until you can touch them with your hands. The charred skin should peel off easily. Any stubborn spots can be removed by scraping with a knife. It is not necessary to peel away all the skin, just most of it. Discard skin. Place peppers into a bowl so that you collect any oils and juices that continue to ooze out—this is all flavor you want to save. If you are preparing a mixed grill, throw the peppers on the fire at the last minute to heat them up and to give them some grill marks and color.

Makes 1 cup.

Note To store, leave peppers in bowl, soak with additional olive oil, cover, and leave in a cool place for up to several weeks.

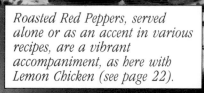

Roasted Red Peppers, served alone or as an accent in various recipes, are a vibrant accompaniment, as here with Lemon Chicken (see page 22).

Base a party menu around the foods of summer. The availability of fresh corn depends on where you live: In New England it is knee-high at the Fourth of July.

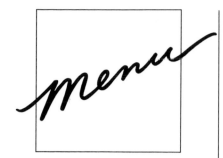

A SUMMER CELEBRATION

*Fresh Basil, Tomato,
and Cucumber Salad*

Andouille-Stuffed Chicken Roll

Grilled Corn (see page 34)

Garlic Roasted Potatoes

*Hot Crusty French Bread
and unsalted butter*

Shortbread and Berries

*Beverage Suggestions:
Cranberry Spritzers and
white Zinfandel*

*When spring drifts into
summer and the days grow
hot, the cooling night makes
the outdoor barbecue a
special event. Fruit stands
announce the season with a
plethora of fresh berries in
early July. Strawberries,
boysenberries, blackberries,
dewberries—each region has
its own treasured berry.
Fresh corn on the cob begins
appearing in the markets
about then too, usually
shipped in from California
or Mexico. What better
way to celebrate the onset of
summer than a festive
grill feast using the new
foods of the season?
All recipes serve 4 to 6.*

PREPARATION PLAN

A great deal of the work for this party menu can be done in advance, freeing you for the day's festivities. Start the day before by baking the shortbread, boning the chicken, roasting the peppers, and preparing the basil-tomato-cucumber salad. The morning of your barbecue, prepare the corn for grilling and put it in water to soak, wash the berries for dessert, make the juice, prepare the garlic potatoes to the point of putting them in the oven, and stuff and tie the chicken roast. Two hours before eating, start the fire and preheat the oven. When the fire is ready, place chicken roll on grill and garlic potatoes in oven. A half hour later, start the corn over direct heat and put the wine in the refrigerator to chill. The potatoes, which will be done first, can be kept warm in the oven until serving time. Spritz the juice just before serving. The only real last-minute chore is to whip the cream for the berries—try to find a young volunteer for that after-dinner duty.

CRANBERRY SPRITZERS

Fresh or frozen concentrate of grapefruit, orange, or raspberry juice works well in this interesting nonalcoholic cocktail. Try combinations of different fruit juices and garnishes, too.

    4 cups cranberry juice
       Ice cubes
    4 cups salt-free seltzer
    2 limes, for garnish

Place juice and ice cubes in a 2-quart pitcher. Stir well. Add seltzer. Thinly slice limes. Top individual glass rims with limes, for garnish.

Makes 8 cups.

FRESH BASIL, TOMATO, AND CUCUMBER SALAD

If you are a tomato gardener, consider growing basil as well. They both fare well in full sun or partial shade and prefer moderately rich soil that is kept lightly moist. If purchasing tomatoes, choose the very freshest, plumpest ripe ones that you can find. Allow this salad to marinate overnight. Don't add salt or pepper ahead of time. Let your guests season to their own tastes. The flavors get more intense the longer they have to meld, making this an ideal choice for a picnic or any time you need a good make-ahead salad.

    2 large cucumbers
    4 large tomatoes
    1 sweet red onion
    ½ bunch fresh basil
    1½ to 2 cups distilled
       white vinegar

1. If cucumbers are waxed, peel them. If not, wash and score lengthwise with a fork around the circumference of cucumber to create an attractive design. Slice into ¼-inch-thick rounds.

2. Wash tomatoes and remove stems. Slice into ¼-inch-thick rounds.

3. Peel onion, slice into ⅛-inch-thick rounds. Reserve.

4. Stem basil, wash, and pat dry. Chop half of the basil coarsely. Reserve remainder for garnish.

5. Arrange onions, tomatoes, and cucumbers in serving bowl. Sprinkle with chopped basil and cover with vinegar. Cover and refrigerate at least 3 hours, preferably overnight.

6. Before serving, drain off most of the liquid. Garnish with remaining basil. Serve well chilled.

Serves 4 to 6.

ANDOUILLE-STUFFED CHICKEN ROLL

Garlicky Cajun-style *andouille* mixed with sweet, freshly roasted red and yellow bell peppers makes a delicious stuffing for a whole boneless chicken. This unusual dish is a perfect choice for entertaining: It can be prepared for grilling a day in advance and makes a stunning table presentation. If andouille is not available in your local market, substitute a high-quality smoked sausage such as kielbasa. If you don't have time to bone a whole chicken, boneless chicken breast can be substituted. Simply reduce the cooking time to 30 to 45 minutes.

2   red bell peppers
2   yellow bell peppers
1   whole chicken (4½ lb), boned
2   tablespoons olive oil
1   teaspoon minced garlic
    Salt, to taste
¾   pound andouille sausage
    Butcher's string
    Oil, for grill
1   lemon, juiced

1. Roast red and yellow peppers. Peel and seed red peppers (see Roasted Red Peppers, page 38); just seed the yellow peppers—peeling is unnecessary. Cut all peppers into ½-inch-wide strips. Chill and reserve.

2. Rub chicken thoroughly with olive oil and garlic. Lay chicken flat on cutting board, skin side down. Lightly salt chicken and try to smooth flesh down to an equal thickness. This is important so that the chicken will cook evenly.

3. Cut each sausage in half lengthwise. Lay half the sausage lengthwise one quarter inch inside right edge of chicken and the other half one quarter inch inside left edge.

4. Spread roasted peppers over entire surface of chicken.

5. Tightly roll each side of chicken until they meet in the center. Tie with butcher's string about every 2 inches. Set aside until grilling time.

6. Prepare fire for indirect-heat method of cooking (see page 12). When fire is ready, place chicken on oiled grill over coals. Sear on all sides, about 8 minutes per side, and then place over drip pan to finish cooking. Close lid. Turn occasionally, and moisten chicken with lemon juice after each turn. Chicken is done when juices run slightly pink to clear (about 1 hour), or when an instant-read thermometer reads 165° F. Remove string and slice to serve.

Serves 4 to 6.

GARLIC ROASTED POTATOES

The bounty of this dish is simplicity. The thinly sliced potatoes become beautifully crisp with a delicious bubbling crust. You can prepare the potatoes ahead of time, leaving only the roasting for the last minute. The olive oil coating will keep the potatoes from turning brown. For a variation try adding chopped fresh herbs to the potatoes. This dish is also an excellent accompaniment to grilled fish.

4   pounds new potatoes
3   tablespoons olive oil
1   tablespoon minced garlic
    Salt and pepper, to taste
4   tablespoons unsalted butter

1. Preheat oven to 450° F.

2. Scrub potatoes and pat dry. Slice into very thin rounds. The thinner the slice, the better these will taste.

3. Place potatoes on baking sheet. Coat completely with olive oil, then sprinkle with garlic, salt, and pepper. Dot with butter.

4. Roast in oven, turning slices every 10 minutes or so to allow for even browning. Potatoes are done when golden brown, about 30 minutes.

Serves 4 to 6.

SHORTBREAD AND BERRIES

Shortbread is a buttery cookie that provides a delicious contrast in texture to freshly whipped cream and fresh berries. Soak the shortbread in cream or berry juices to soften it a bit, or let your guests do this for themselves at the table. An interesting variation is to substitute pecans for almonds.

1   pound softened butter, plus
    butter for preparing pan
4   cups flour, plus flour
    for dusting
1   cup sugar
4   ounces ground almonds
3   egg whites
2   teaspoons vanilla extract
2   cups fresh berries
¼   cup sugar (optional)
1   pint heavy cream

1. Preheat oven to 275° F. Butter and lightly flour a baking sheet.

2. In a large bowl cream the 1 pound butter and the 1 cup sugar with electric mixer at medium speed until light and fluffy (about 5 minutes). Use a paddle attachment on your mixer if you have one.

3. In a small bowl, mix the 4 cups flour and ground almonds. Slowly add flour mixture to butter mixture, about ¼ cup at a time.

4. Whip egg whites until slightly frothy. Fold egg whites and vanilla into batter by hand until just mixed. Spread mixture evenly onto prepared pan. Bake until lightly browned on top (about 50 minutes). Cool on wire rack. Place in storage container only after completely cooled if shortbread is made a day prior to serving.

5. Wash, stem, and slice berries. If you lightly sprinkle berries with the ¼ cup sugar and refrigerate for a few hours, they will soften and make their own delicious juice to pour on your shortbread. Whip the cream. Serve shortbread at room temperature with whipped cream and berries.

Serves 4 to 6.

...FOR BONING A WHOLE CHICKEN

A boneless chicken provides a showy and unusual focal point for your next dinner party. Once you have mastered this boning technique, let your imagination run wild creating different dishes by using a variety of stuffings. The finished product makes a beautiful presentation and can be sliced at the table into attractive rondelles.

2. *Separate the thighbone from the backbone. Cut the cartilage between the breastbone and the backbone. Separate the wings from the breastbone and remove wing bones. Peel the meat off the thighbone and remove the thighbone.*

4. *Flip the bird over and cut a complete circle around the foot end of each leg bone to loosen the flesh. Scrape the leg bone with your knife in a circular motion to push back the flesh. Flip the bird over again and finish removing the leg bone.*

1. *Wash chicken and pat dry. Place breast side down on cutting board. Begin by cutting to the bone down the center of the backbone from neck to tail. Pick up the skin next to the neck with one hand and pull the skin away from the bone. With your other hand, use the boning knife to separate the meat from the bone. Continue to use this method to peel the meat and skin away from both sides of the backbone. Be careful not to puncture the skin.*

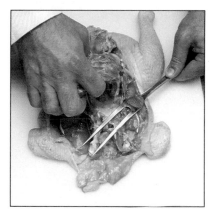

3. *Follow the curvature of the ribs with your knife, exposing the rib bones. Follow the rib bones fully around to the keel bone and make a horizontal cut along the keel bone. Firmly grab the rib cage, pulling up to remove the breastbone. Carefully remove the remaining keel bone without puncturing the skin.*

5. *Spread out the boned chicken and flatten the meat to form an even surface by moving parts of the reserved dark meat to areas of skin that are bare. Butterfly the thickest part of the breast meat and flatten the entire surface with the back of your knife or with a mallet. Place the stuffing in the center of the bird. Roll, tie with butcher's string, and grill as directed in the Andouille-Stuffed Chicken Roll recipe on the opposite page.*

A domed, kettle-shaped water smoker is the perfect tool for home smoking, although both kettle-shaped grills and gas grills can be adapted for the job.

Smoking

Where there is fire, there is smoke. People have long been enjoying smoked food; our cave-dwelling ancestors were the first smokers of meat and fish. Smoking became an important part of food preservation and flavoring in the eighteenth, nineteenth, and early twentieth centuries before the advent of refrigeration and canning. Smoking today is not done to preserve, but to add a delicious smoky flavor to foods. This chapter provides instruction for producing smoked meats, fish, shellfish, poultry, and vegetables in a quick—and not salty—fashion in your home using a piece of equipment called a water smoker. Recipes are also provided for dishes that include purchased smoked foods.

... FOR COLD SMOKING

Recipes in this section were designed for use with a home-style water smoker. Always set up your water smoker outside, out of reach of children and pets. Watch the wind, too; avoid sending hours of smoke—however aromatic—into your home or your neighbor's.

1. *Set up water smoker outside. Remove top and center ring. Open bottom vents halfway. Put 6 cups hardwood sawdust in a pan or cast-iron pot placed on the bottom grill inside the smoker. Place ½ cup hardwood sawdust in a 6- to 8-inch skillet and heat over high heat on a portable hot plate or burner. This must be done outside. After a minute the sawdust will begin to smolder.*

2. *When all sawdust has blackened (some will contain minute glowing embers and some will be covered in gray ash), remove pan from heat and dump burning sawdust on top of sawdust set up inside smoker.*

3. *Replace center ring on top of the bottom section. Place water pan in position without water to catch any fat or juices. Replace top grill and arrange food in a single layer. Replace lid and partially close vent. Insert instant-read thermometer into vent. The temperature should stay between 90° F and 130° F.*

4. *Every 2 to 3 hours, gently stir the sawdust in the pot. Make sure that smoke is gently rising out of the vents. If not, add more sawdust, making sure to stir ashes over the new sawdust.*

When you use a smoker overnight, it is not necessary to lose sleep tending it. Before you go to bed, make sure the sawdust pan is full of fresh sawdust and well lit. The next morning stir the embers. If they have gone out, remove ashes and fill the pan with fresh sawdust. Repeat the procedure for starting the sawdust, and continue smoking.

SMOKING DEFINED

Smoking is a food-preparation process in which fat- and water-soluble molecules, steam, and microscopic particles are released from burning wood and deposited on the surface of food placed in a smoker. The natural moisture in food absorbs the smoke flavors, which eventually diffuse from the surface of the food into the interior to give the food a wonderful smoky flavor. Smoking also dries out the food. Drying concentrates the flavors and changes texture and appearance. By decreasing the moisture in food, smoking also helps to preserve it. The smoking recipes in this chapter include those for cold smoking (a flavoring method but not a true cooking method) and for smoke cooking (a method which truly cooks food). Neither of these methods should be considered an adequate means of food preservation.

Cold Smoking

Cold smoking is the type of smoking common on plantations and country homes in the last two centuries. The term *cold* is misleading since it is by no means cold in the smokehouses. Cold smoking is "cold" only in the sense that it is done at cooler temperatures than smoke cooking. In general, cold smoking is done between 90° F and 130° F. At these temperatures food is not cooked, although it may be dried by the process. Traditionally, highly salted meats were smoked in special houses or in the chimneys of large country fireplaces. They were smoked for days or even weeks, and although the temperature was insufficient to cook the food, the heavy smoke and high salt content discouraged the growth of bacteria, molds, and other fungi. Today this style of smoked food lives on as a flavoring method, most commonly used to produce country or "Virginia" hams, lox, some types of sausages, and bacon. Cold smoking can be done successfully at home by using a kettle-shaped, covered water smoker, as the recipes in this chapter for cold smoking illustrate. The recipes begin on page 54.

Cold-smoked Pork Butt Bacon (see page 55) adds a rich accent to a traditional breakfast. Although smoked, the meat must be cooked again before eating.

Beautiful, golden Smoked Chicken (see page 56) is a classic example of smoke cooking. This recipe merits being a staple in your cooking repertoire since its uses are practically endless. Delicious either hot or cold, serve it whole, as seen here, or boned and added to cold salads and sandwiches.

SMOKING EQUIPMENT

Gas or electric smokers are small versions of the type of smoker used commercially. All smokers consist of a metal box with a heating element on the bottom. A pan holds smoldering wood chips or hardwood sawdust over the element. Food is held on a rack or suspended on hooks. By paying careful attention to temperature and heat source, you can use these smokers for both cold smoking and smoke cooking. If you want to try cold smoking, follow the instructions for cold smoking as adapted for the water smoker (see page 46). If you want to smoke cook, follow the basic guidelines presented on the opposite page and the manufacturer's instructions provided with your smoker. Gas and electric smokers were not tested for this book. Instead, all recipes were tested using a kettle-shaped covered water smoker. However, these recipes can be adapted for gas and electric smokers. Consult your instruction manual for details.

Homemade Smokers

These may be as simple as an oil drum, a garbage can, or an old refrigerator, or they may be as elaborate as a brick smokehouse. Like the commercial variety, homemade smokers consist of a heat source (such as a hot plate), a pan to hold chips or sawdust, and racks or poles from which to suspend the food. These smokers are particularly suitable for cold smoking, but using them for smoke cooking can sometimes be difficult because consistent high temperatures cannot be maintained. You may prefer to smoke the food first and then finish the cooking in a kitchen oven set to 200° F to 250° F. These types of smokers were not tested for use with the recipes in this book.

Smoke Cooking

Smoke cooking, also called hot smoking, refers to smoking at temperatures high enough to cook the food that is being smoked. Usually, smoke cooking is done at a temperature between 150° F and 250° F. Smoke cooking at home has become quite popular since the advent of the kettle-shaped, covered water smoker. The recipes in this chapter for smoke cooking were designed to use this type of water smoker. More information on this equipment is provided on page 50. Smoke cooking recipes begin on page 55.

. . . FOR SMOKE COOKING

Recipes in this book for smoke cooking (also called hot smoking) were designed for use with a kettle-shaped, covered, home-style water smoker. Consult the chart on page 59 to determine how many charcoal briquettes and how much wood to use and the cooking time for each type of food. All smoke cooking must be done outside, out of reach of children and pets. Be careful of wind, which may blow the smoke into your house or—worse—your neighbor's.

1. Set up water smoker outside. Remove the top and center ring and open all vents. Start charcoal briquettes in a charcoal chimney, or place them directly on bottom grill inside ring and start with an electric starter. Coals are ready when coated with a light gray ash (about 30 minutes). Spread coals evenly across the inside of the charcoal ring. Place water pan in position and fill with desired hot liquid. Set lower grill over water pan. Carefully set middle ring in place on top of the bottom section.

Soak 2- by 3-inch wood chunks of choice in water for at least 1 hour. Shake off excess water. Open side door and, using tongs, place wood on top of coals. Consult the chart on page 59, and start with the least amount of wood recommended.

2. Preparation of food for smoke cooking varies with the recipe. Some foods need to be coated with spices or a marinade; others are brushed with oil before being placed in the water smoker. Set cooking racks in place and add food in a single layer. Leave an inch or two between pieces of food so smoke can circulate. If cooking different foods with varying cooking times, place the food that will be done first on the top racks. Remember that foods above will drip on foods below, so do not allow foods to drip if the flavors are incompatible.

Partially close all vents while smoke cooking. Use oven mitts or hot pads when adjusting vents. Insert instant-read thermometer into top vent. After 30 minutes the thermometer should read at least 170°F. The ideal range is between 170°F and 250°F. Remember: The water smoker functions best when not nursed.

3. Try not to open the lid of the water smoker while you're cooking. After 3½ to 4 hours, you will probably need to add more hot water to the water pan. The pan should always be at least half full. For longer periods of smoking, you will need to add more briquettes and possibly more wood. Add a dozen or so briquettes every 1½ hours.

If the smoker is not maintaining sufficient heat (at least 170° F), open the vents. If the fire is dying out, open the front door of the smoker. The additional oxygen will get the fire going again. If the smoker is still too cool, add more briquettes.

If the temperature is too hot (above 250° F), try closing the vents more. If this doesn't work, add some cold water to the water pan or remove some of the briquettes.

4. Smoke-cooked meat is often pink below the outer surface, so rely on temperature. See page 59 or the individual recipes for a rough guide to internal temperatures of cooked meat. Insert the thermometer into the thickest part of the food, making sure it does not touch bone.

Smoked Beef Brisket With Barbecue Sauce (see page 55) is an ideal choice for first-time home water smoker users because you can hardly fail to turn out a superb meal. The smoke cooking method calls for a slow cooking time of five to eight hours, but the meat can be left virtually unattended. Just maintain the temperature of the water smoker and you will be rewarded with juicy, tender meat. Heated Louisiana Sauce (see page 80) is ready to pour over the beef just out of the smoker although any tomato-based barbecue sauce can be served with the meat.

Water Smokers

In recent years water smokers have become widely available and are quite popular for home use. Most use charcoal briquettes as the heat source, but gas or electric models exist. All recipes in this chapter were prepared in a charcoal-fired water smoker, which has a domed top and looks like an elongated barbecue kettle. At the bottom is a fire pan for charcoal and wood. Above the heat source is a water pan and one or two grills to hold the food. Most water smokers are versatile enough to also serve as a covered barbecue grill, steamer, open braiser, and an oven for dry roasting. The model used for testing these recipes also had a side door that allowed access for replenishing charcoal, wood, and liquid with ease and minimal heat loss.

Water smokers work by creating a dense, steam-filled smoky fog that both smokes and cooks the food with moist heat. Basting is not necessary. The moisture transforms large, tough cuts of meat such as beef briskets into roasts that are juicy and tender. The addition of water, aromatic liquids, wine, or beer gives water-smoked food a flavor quality not produced by other types of smokers. Another advantage to using a water smoker is that it can hold food for up to an hour after it is cooked without drying it. However, food cooked in a water smoker does not develop the crusty exterior that dry roasting produces.

The exact method of use varies for each brand of water smoker, so consult the manufacturer's instructions for specifics about how many charcoal briquettes and how much water and wood to use.

WOOD FOR SMOKING

Hardwoods are good for all types of smoking. Softwoods—such as pine, fir, cedar, and spruce—are not suitable because they give off pitch and resin. These substances give food a turpentinelike flavor and coat everything with a black, sticky film. If you cannot identify the wood you are about to use for smoking, do not use it. Never use plant clippings that may contain insecticides or poisonous plants such as oleander. The most popular woods for smoking are hickory, fruitwoods, mahogany, mesquite, and oak. Dried corncobs also make good smoke fuel.

Different woods impart different flavors to the food being smoked. Some woods work better with fish and others work better with pork. Refer to the chart on page 59 for some suggestions about combinations of wood and food, but remember: Taste is personal. Experiment with woods that suit your own taste.

For smoke cooking use chunks of wood. These should be soaked first so that they smolder and do not burn. You can use chips of wood, but you will have to replace them more frequently.

ACCURACY IN SMOKING

Smoking is not an exact science, and no smoking recipe in this chapter is meant to be exact. There are too many variables involved in the smoking process to allow for precise instruction and complete reproducibility. The temperature of the meat, the outside air temperature, the humidity, the thickness of the meat, the density of the cut, the type of smoke, the amount of food in the smoker, and the temperature of the smoker are some of the variables that cannot be completely controlled.

Do not fear, however. It is easy to achieve excellent results from smoking recipes every time as long as you pay attention to the temperature of the food as it is smoking. To do this, you need an accurate thermometer. Purchase what is known as an instant-read (or microwave) thermometer (see page 7). Do not use a traditional meat thermometer; it is not always accurate. Remember that instant-read thermometers are made of plastic and cannot be left in the food while it is cooking. It is also a good idea to have a second instant-read thermometer to set in the top vent of the smoker (if your water smoker did not come with a built-in thermometer) to monitor the temperature of the smoker itself.

Recording Information

Keep your own records and develop the best methods to suit your own taste. Maintain a journal of your smoking experiences that is similar to the chart on page 59. If you keep track of the important variables, you will be able to reproduce your successful results and eliminate the possibility of making the same mistake twice. Here is a list of variables you should keep track of in your journal: Meat Weight, Ingredients of Cure, Length of Time in Cure, Type of Wood Used, Smoking Time and Temperature, Outside Air Temperature, Temperature of Meat When Finished, and Other Comments (such as How Did I Like It?).

... FOR SAFE SMOKING

Common sense is your best guide to safe smoking. Never attempt to smoke foods indoors, and follow the guidelines in Tips for Safe Grilling (see page 10). Also read the instructions included with your equipment for any safety information concerning your specific brand of smoker.

☐ Smoking is to be done outside only. Never smoke foods indoors—fumes produced can be lethal. Do not use gasoline, alcohol, or any other highly flammable liquid to ignite charcoal briquettes.

☐ Avoid using commercial lighter fluid or charcoal briquettes that have been impregnated with lighter fluid as they can impart an unpleasant taste to the smoked food.

☐ Never pour water directly onto hot coals. This will give off dust and soot that will coat the food.

☐ There are many variables that affect the smoking process. Some you cannot control, such as weather and altitude. To be on the safe side, always allow extra cooking time (30 minutes to 1 hour extra is usually adequate).

☐ Experiment with different woods and flavor enhancers, such as herb branches, mint leaves, and orange and lemon rinds.

☐ Set up the smoker away from the house on a level heatproof surface. You do not want the smoker near the house since the aroma of smoke can linger. Keep out of the way of general traffic. Warn children to keep away. The smoker becomes very hot during use.

☐ Always cook with the cover closed on the smoker.

☐ Use oven mitts or hot pads when handling the hot smoker.

☐ Turn food with long-handled tongs instead of a fork to prevent piercing the meats and losing flavorful juices.

☐ During smoking look at food only when absolutely necessary. Although it is tempting to check the progress, every time the lid is lifted, you need to add 15 minutes to the cooking time.

☐ Replace lid and close all vents when finished cooking to allow fire to burn itself out over time. Do not use water to extinguish coals because water may damage the finish of the smoker.

☐ Remove ashes from bottom frequently. You may wish to cover the sides of the water pan with foil since grease tends to build up on both the inside and outside. It is not necessary to wash the inside of the smoker. The outside may be washed, if you wish, with a sudsy sponge and rinsed with warm water. Avoid harsh cleaners that may damage the exterior finish of your equipment. Touch-up scratches to prevent rust.

. . . OF BRINES

The brining of meat and fish before smoking provides the salty flavor characteristic of many smoked foods. Brine, also called wet cure or pickle, is a solution of salt, water, sugar, and—often—sodium nitrite. Meat placed in a brine solution cures by having its moisture content reduced and the moisture replaced with salt. The addition of sodium nitrite to the brine not only gives the meat the traditional pink color but retards the growth of botulism.

Nitrite need be present in cures only if the meat will be subject to prolonged cold smoking (longer than 3 to 4 hours). During cold smoking the temperature is ideal for bacterial growth. Nitrite does not need to be used for meat that will be smoke cooked since the temperature is high enough to cook the food before bacterial growth can occur. Spices and other flavoring can be added to the brine for additional flavor.

Sodium Nitrite

The United States Department of Agriculture, which oversees the commercial processing of meat, requires that only 6.1 grams of sodium nitrite be used to cure 100 pounds of meat. When smoking small batches of meat at home, the proportionate amount of sodium nitrite is so small that it is difficult to measure accurately. As a result, the home cook usually buys a commercial preparation in which sodium nitrite has been cut with other substances such as salt and dextrose. Figure that instead of 6.1 grams, 4 ounces of this sodium mixture is used to cure 100 pounds of meat.

These curing salts are sold under brand names like Prague Powder and Ham Cure, and the products can be purchased from butcher-supply houses or through mail-order sources (see page 121).

Curing Times

Many variables affect the timing of the curing process. The three most important are the strength of the cure (how salty it is), the temperature during curing, and the thickness of the piece of meat to be cured. In commercial operations needles are inserted into large pieces of meat, and brine is pumped under pressure through the needles into the meat. This speeds curing and aids in the distribution of the cure. Most home cooks do not have injection needles and pumps, however, and must rely on the old-fashioned method of passive diffusion. Passive diffusion works fine for smaller cuts of meat. The curing of large pieces of meat, such as whole hams, is beyond the scope of this book.

The curing times given in the individual recipes are only guidelines. Keep records of results in a journal (see page 51), and adjust the timing of subsequent efforts to suit your taste. If the meat is too salty, decrease the curing time. If not salty enough, increase the curing time. Remember: If curing takes longer than 2 hours, do it in the refrigerator.

BASIC BRINE

This recipe is good for bacon, pork loins, and hams. Follow these steps for the other brine recipes that do not list instructions as well.

- *1 gallon water*
- *1½ cups kosher salt*
- *1 cup sugar (granulated or firmly packed brown)*
- *4 ounces curing salt (sodium nitrite mixture)*

Place the water in a 2-gallon non-aluminum, non-cast iron container. Add salt and sugar, stirring continuously until completely dissolved. Add curing salt and stir until dissolved. Submerge meat in liquid and place a heavy plate on top to keep it completely submerged. If meat is to be cured for more than 3 days, overhaul brine. To do this, remove meat. Stir brine, making sure that undissolved particles dissolve. Replace meat and weigh down with a heavy plate.

CHINESE BRINE FOR DUCK OR CHICKEN

- *1 gallon water*
- *1½ cups kosher salt*
- *1 cup sugar*
- *½ cup light soy sauce*
- *1 teaspoon Chinese five-spice powder*
- *2 slices fresh ginger*

SPICY BRINE FOR BEEF, LAMB, PORK, OR VEAL

The photograph at right features Smoked Pork Chops in Spicy Brine (see page 60) combined with Smoked Winter Squash With Maple Syrup (see page 63) for an autumn supper that is sure to become a family favorite.

- *1 gallon water*
- *1½ cups kosher salt*
- *1 cup sugar*
- *2 teaspoons cayenne pepper*
- *2 tablespoons pepper*
- *2 tablespoons cumin seed*
- *1 teaspoon whole thyme, oregano, or basil leaves*
- *1 tablespoon garlic, minced*

FISH BRINE

- *1 gallon water*
- *1½ cups kosher salt*
- *½ cup soy sauce*
- *1 cup sugar*
- *2 bay leaves*
- *1 teaspoon dried dill or 4 sprigs fresh dill*
- *Zest of 2 lemons*

LAMB AND VENISON BRINE

- *1 gallon water*
- *1¼ cup kosher salt*
- *½ cup soy sauce*
- *1 cup sugar*
- *2 tablespoons mustard seed*
- *6 whole allspice berries, crushed*
- *1 tablespoon dried summer savory*
- *2 tablespoons minced garlic*

AROMATIC BRINE FOR PORK, DUCK, OR CHICKEN

> 1 gallon water
> 2 cups kosher salt
> 1 cup firmly packed
>   brown sugar
> ½ cup molasses
> 2 tablespoons black pepper
> ⅔ cup crushed fennel seed
> 1 tablespoon dried sage
>   Zest of 1 tangerine
>   Rind of 1 lemon

CORNED BEEF OR PASTRAMI BRINE

The brine for pastrami must be cooked to bring out the flavor of the pickling spice.

> 1 gallon water
> 2 cups kosher salt
> 1 cup sugar
> ¼ cup pickling spice
> 1 tablespoon granulated garlic
> 2 tablespoons cracked
>   peppercorns
> 8 bay leaves
> 4 ounces curing salt
>   (sodium nitrite), optional

In a 2-gallon non-aluminum pot, combine the water, salt, sugar, pickling spice, garlic, peppercorns, bay leaves, and curing salt (if used). Bring to a boil and stir until salts and sugar are dissolved. Cover pot and reduce heat to a simmer. Cook 20 minutes. Remove from heat and cool to room temperature. Refrigerate until cold, about 2 hours. This can be done ahead of time. Add meat as described for Pastrami (see page 65)

. . . AND DRY CURES

A dry cure is a mixture of salt, sugar, and, sometimes, sodium nitrite that is rubbed directly on meat or fish. It is the traditional method used to cure country hams and bacon. You may find it difficult to control the saltiness of the final product, especially on larger cuts of meat such as hams. For home use the dry-cure method is most suitable for smaller pieces of food, such as fish fillets and pork bellies.

All dry cures are made in the same manner. In a small plastic container, combine ingredients. Cover and shake to mix.

BASIC DRY CURE

> 2 cups kosher salt
> 1 cup firmly packed
>   brown sugar
> 2 ounces curing salt
>   (sodium nitrite mixture)
> 4 tablespoons black pepper

FISH DRY CURE

> 2 cups kosher salt
> ¼ cup sugar
> 1 tablespoon pepper
> 1 teaspoon dried dill
> 1 teaspoon dried oregano

Breakfast featuring Smoked Salmon has an international character despite being an American invention. Cream cheese was first developed in New York state in 1920. Serving cream cheese, smoked salmon, and the traditional staple bread of Jewish immigrants—the bagel—in the morning was started in New York City within the last 50 years. Cappuccino, which is a combination of strong coffee and steamed milk, derives from Italy.

RECIPES FOR COLD SMOKING

These classic cold-smoked foods can be purchased in delis throughout the country, but they are infinitely better made fresh in your own backyard.

SMOKED PORK LOIN (CANADIAN BACON)

Once smoked the pork is not fully cooked but can be roasted to an internal temperature of 150° F or sliced and fried as Canadian bacon. Roasted pork loins are also good cold in sandwiches.

- 2 boneless center-cut pork loin (4 to 6 lb each)
- 1 recipe Basic Brine (see page 52)

Smoked Pork Loin is left whole and prepared in exactly the same way as Pork Butt Bacon (see opposite page). Depending on the thickness of the loin, it will require 3 to 5 days to cure. Follow all instructions for Pork Butt Bacon. If curing for more than 3 days, don't forget to overhaul the cure (see page 53 for instructions).

Makes 7 to 10 pounds pork loin.

SMOKED SALMON

Unlike commercial smoked salmon, which has a high salt content to give it a long shelf life, home-smoked salmon need not be nearly as salty. Have the fishmonger prepare the salmon side by removing as many bones as possible. Be prepared with needle-nose pliers to remove any small bones that may remain. This same recipe can be used for other large fish of the same size, such as sturgeon and sea bass.

- 1 side fresh salmon (3 to 4 lb), skin attached
- 1 recipe Fish Dry Cure (see page 53)
- ¼ cup oil, plus oil, for brushing

1. Wash salmon thoroughly. Remove small bones with pliers. Sprinkle ⅛-inch layer of Fish Dry Cure on a baking sheet or piece of aluminum foil large enough to hold salmon. Then place fish, skin side down, on pan or foil. Sprinkle fish, including tail, with ⅛-inch layer of dry cure. (Use less cure on the tail, which is thinner, so that it doesn't become too salty.) Cover with plastic wrap and refrigerate for 2 to 5 hours; time depends on the thickness of fish and saltiness desired. Be sure to keep notes for future reference.

2. Remove fish from refrigerator, uncover, wash, and pat dry. Place on a wire rack (such as a cake rack) in front of an electric fan so that air circulates above and below fish. Let salmon dry until dry to the touch and a thin skin (called the pellicle) has formed (about 6 hours). Brush lightly with oil.

3. Prepare water smoker for cold smoking (see page 46). Place salmon, skin side down, on top grill. Smoke at no more than 110° F for 3 to 6 hours. Periodically stir sawdust and add more as needed. Remove fish and let cool to room temperature. Wrap in plastic wrap and refrigerate. When completely cooled, cut on the slant into thin slices. Well-wrapped smoked salmon keeps for a week refrigerated. It can also be frozen but the texture will be somewhat mushy.

Makes 30 slices.

COUNTRY-STYLE DRY-CURED BACON

Dry-cured bacon was the traditional bacon of the plantations and farms of early America. In Virginia and other southern states, it is still made this way. Dry-cured bacon will keep refrigerated two to three weeks or for two months if frozen. Remember that the bacon is not fully cooked after smoking; you must cook it again before eating.

1 whole pork belly (8 to 10 lb)
1 recipe Basic Dry Cure
   (see page 53)

1. Trim pork belly so edges are square. Cut belly in half so that it fits on the smoker. Rub about half the dry cure mixture into all sides and edges of both pieces of meat and reserve remaining mixture. Place pieces into a heavy-duty plastic bag, one skin side down and the other on top of it so the skin side is up. Seal the bag and place into a pan large enough to hold the belly pieces. Refrigerate for a total of 4 days. After 1 or 2 days, meat juices and dry cure form a natural brine. Turn the bag over each day. After the fourth day remove belly pieces, discard liquid, and rub meat with reserved dry cure. Return belly to the plastic bag and continue to cure another 4 to 6 days, turning the bag over each day.

2. Remove meat from the plastic bag, wash, and pat dry. Place meat on a wire rack (such as a cake rack) or tie with string and suspend meat from a pole in front of an electric fan so that air circulates around it. Let meat dry until surface is no longer tacky to the touch (16 to 24 hours).

3. Prepare water smoker for cold smoking (see page 46). Place meat into smoker, skin side down on the grill. Cover and smoke at no higher than 120° F for at least 6 hours and up to 24 hours. Periodically stir sawdust and add more as needed.

4. Remove bacon, let cool to room temperature, and wrap before refrigerating. Well wrapped, refrigerated bacon will keep for 2 to 3 weeks.

Makes 6 to 8 pounds bacon.

PORK BUTT BACON

Pork butt makes a lean and delicious bacon. These chunks can also be roasted whole with a sweet sugar or honey glaze, just like ham. Once roasted, the bacon can be eaten hot or cold. This pork is not fully cooked after the smoking process; it must be cooked before it can be eaten. Either slice and fry as you would bacon or roast whole to an internal temperature of 155° F to 165° F.

2 pork butts (5 to 6 lb each)
1 recipe Basic Brine, with
   sodium nitrite (see page 52)

1. Have a butcher remove bone from pork butts. Cut each butt into 4 to 6 large chunks of approximately equal size. Prepare brine. Place meat into a non-aluminum container. Cover with brine. Weight down meat with a heavy plate so that the pieces stay submerged. Refrigerate for 1 to 2 days. To test if meat is completely cured, cut a chunk in half and check color. Cured meat is uniformly pink all the way through.

2. Remove meat from cure and discard cure. Wash meat and pat dry. Place meat on a wire rack (such as a cake rack) or tie with string and suspend from a pole and use an electric fan to circulate air around meat. Let meat dry until surface is dry to the touch, 16 to 24 hours.

3. Prepare water smoker for cold smoking (see page 46). Place meat on grill. Cover and smoke at no greater than 130° F for at least 6 hours or overnight. Periodically stir sawdust and add more as needed. Remove meat from smoker. Cool to room temperature before refrigerating. Well-wrapped Pork Butt Bacon will keep 1 to 2 weeks refrigerated or up to 2 months in the freezer.

Makes 8 to 10 pounds bacon.

RECIPES FOR SMOKE COOKING

More than merely a flavoring, this method actually cooks food. Remember, however, that smoke cooking is not a method of food preservation. Think of it as having the same effect as roasting in the oven.

SMOKED BEEF BRISKET WITH BARBECUE SAUCE

The water smoker must have been invented to cook briskets. This tough cut of meat comes out juicy and tender with a wonderful smoky flavor. Leftover brisket can be rewarmed by slicing and simmering in your favorite tomato-based barbecue sauce (see page 80) over low heat for 10 minutes.

1 beef brisket (8 lb)
3 cloves garlic, minced
1 tablespoon salt
1 teaspoon black pepper
2 teaspoons paprika
½ teaspoon each cayenne pepper,
   dried thyme, and ground
   cumin
1 teaspoon dried mustard
2 cups tomato-based barbecue
   sauce (see page 80)

1. Wash brisket. Trim away large chunks of fat, leaving at least a ¼-inch-thick layer of fat. Rub garlic and salt all over brisket. Combine black pepper, paprika, cayenne, thyme, cumin, and mustard; rub mixture over brisket to coat meat. Cover with plastic wrap and let rest at room temperature for 1 to 3 hours.

2. Prepare water smoker for smoke cooking (see page 49). Place brisket, fat side up, on the grill. Cover and smoke cook at a temperature between 200° F and 250° F. Add charcoal briquettes, wood, and water as needed. Brisket is done when internal temperature reaches 160° F to 170° F (after 5 to 8 hours of cooking).

3. Remove meat to a large platter or cutting board. Let rest 15 minutes before slicing. Serve with heated barbecue sauce.

Serves 6 to 8.

SMOKED CHICKEN

It is always a good idea to make more than one bird when using this recipe since there is little additional work involved. You can eat the extra chicken cold (which is just as delicious as the hot version), or use the smoked meat in other dishes such as Smoked Chicken and Fresh Apricot Salad (see page 68).

> 2 *chickens (3½ lb each)*
> 1 *gallon water*
> 1¼ *pounds salt*
> ⅔ *cup sugar*
> ¾ *cup soy sauce*
> 1 *teaspoon* each *dried tarragon dried thyme, and pepper*
> ¼ *cup olive oil*

1. Thoroughly wash birds inside and out. Put the water in a large non-aluminum container and in it dissolve salt, and sugar. Add soy sauce, tarragon, thyme, and pepper. Submerge birds in the brine and weight them down with a heavy plate so they stay submerged. Marinate in refrigerator overnight or at room temperature for 2 hours.

2. Remove birds from brine, wash, and pat dry. Reserve brine. Truss birds for cooking.

3. Prepare water smoker for smoke cooking (see page 49). Fill water pan with hot water and half the reserved brine. Place birds, breast side up, on the grill. Cover and smoke cook at 200° F to 250° F. Add charcoal briquettes, wood, and water as needed. Brush birds with olive oil every 2 hours. Chickens are done when internal temperature of the thickest part of the thigh registers 160° F to 170° F, about 4 hours of cooking time. Remove birds from smoker and let rest 10 minutes. Carve and serve. Well-wrapped leftovers will keep 3 to 5 days refrigerated.

Serves 8.

SMOKED DUCK

The Chinese are the masters of duck cookery. This recipe combines Chinese spicing and flavors with smoke cooking for a fragrant, succulent result. The duck is delicious cold in Chinese Smoked-Duck Salad (see page 69), so make two ducks so that you have leftovers. The cooking temperature given in this recipe will probably produce a slightly less than well-done duck. If you like well-done duck, smoke to an internal temperature of 170° F to 175° F.

> 2 *ducks (4 to 6 lb each)*
> 1 *recipe Chinese Brine for Duck or Chicken (see page 52)*
> 1 *teaspoon Chinese five-spice powder*
> 1 *ginger root (about ¼ lb), sliced into ¼-inch-thick slices*
> 6 *whole star anise, soaked in water for at least 30 minutes*

1. Wash ducks thoroughly inside and out. Place ducks in a large non-aluminum container, cover with brine, and weight birds down with a heavy plate so that they stay submerged. Refrigerate 16 to 20 hours. Remove from brine and reserve brine. Wash ducks and pat dry. Sprinkle cavity of each with five-spice powder. Truss ducks.

2. Prepare water smoker for smoke cooking (see page 49). Put 2 cups reserved brine in the pan, then fill pan with hot water. Place ducks breast side up on the grill. Cover and smoke cook at a temperature between 200° F and 250° F. Add charcoal briquettes, wood, and water as needed. Check the internal temperature of ducks after about 3 hours. When it reaches 150° F, add the ginger root and star anise to the coals. The duck is done when the internal temperature of the meat registers 155° F to 165° F (about 4 hours of cooking). Remove ducks from smoker. Let rest 10 minutes before cutting into quarters with poultry shears and serving.

Each duck serves 4.

SMOKED TROUT

Trout is a fish that takes well to smoke. If you or someone you know is successful at fishing, you may have more trout than you know what to do with. Smoking not only increases the length of time you can keep the trout, but smoked trout can also be frozen. Once smoked, trout will keep refrigerated for 5 to 7 days; smoked and frozen, it will keep for 2 to 3 months. This recipe works well for any small (¾ to 1½ pounds) whole fish, including mackerel, whitefish, and bluefish. Although the fish can be eaten hot, it is especially good cold as an appetizer or light lunch (see Smoked Fish Salad With Lemon-Dill Dressing, page 68).

> 6 to 8 *whole trout (¾ to 1½ lb each), gutted*
> 1 *recipe Fish Brine (see page 52)*
> ½ *cup oil*

1. Place fish in a non-aluminum container. Cover with brine. Place a heavy plate on fish so that they remain submerged. Let rest 45 minutes to 1½ hours, depending on the size of fish and the saltiness you desire. (Experiment and keep notes.) Remove fish from brine, wash, and pat dry.

2. Prepare water smoker for smoke cooking (see page 49). Don't use the water pan. Ideally, the smoker temperature should be maintained between 150° F and 190° F. Brush fish lightly with oil and place on grill. Cover and smoke cook until flesh can just be flaked with a fork, 45 minutes to 1½ hours of cooking. Remove fish from grill and brush with additional oil. Fish can be eaten immediately or allowed to cool to room temperature. If cooled, wrap well, and refrigerate or freeze until use.

Serves 6 to 8.

Master smoke cooking and use Smoked Duck to benefit a wide spectrum of dishes. Recipes using smoked foods include Chinese Smoked-Duck Salad on page 69.

Many types of fish lend themselves to smoking. Here, halibut steaks were used in Smoked Fish Fillets with the Lime-Ginger Marinade recipe for wonderous results. Combine the halibut with shrimp prepared using the method described for Smoked Shellfish on page 61. Once you have learned the smoke cooking and cold smoking techniques, experiment with different food combinations of your own.

SMOKED FISH FILLETS

Halibut, rock cod, shark, sea bass, bluefish, drum, tuna, mahi mahi, spearfish, swordfish, cod, salmon, or sturgeon will work well in this recipe. The main criterion is that the fish is not so delicate that is falls apart during cooking. This recipe gives a choice of two marinade recipes; you can also choose to make this recipe with Fish Brine (see page 52). If you use brine, simply soak the fish in the brine at room temperature for 1 to 2 hours and smoke cook for 1 to 2 hours. Fish prepared in the brine is best eaten cold. Fish prepared with the following marinades is good served hot right out of the smoker or cold as in Smoked Fish Salad With Lemon-Dill Dressing (see page 68).

> 2 pounds fish steaks or
> fish fillets

Lemon and
Fresh Herb Marinade

> Juice of 2 lemons
> ⅓ cup olive oil
> ¼ cup chopped fresh herbs
> (chervil, tarragon, oregano,
> thyme, dill, or fennel)
> 2 teaspoons chopped garlic
> 1 teaspoon each salt and pepper

Lime-Ginger Marinade

> 1 tablespoon minced
> fresh ginger
> Juice of 2 limes
> 2 teaspoons minced garlic
> ¼ cup oil, preferably peanut
> 2 tablespoons each soy sauce
> and Asian sesame oil
> 1 teaspoon salt
> ¼ cup chopped cilantro

1. Wash fish and pat dry. Place fish in a glass or stainless-steel bowl, cover with Lime-Ginger Marinade or Lemon and Fresh Herb Marinade, and let rest at room temperature for 1 to 4 hours. Turn fish once or twice during marinating.

2. Prepare water smoker for smoke cooking (see page 49). Do not use water pan. Remove fish from marinade; reserve marinade. Place fish on the grill, cover, and smoke cook at a constant temperature between 150° F and 210° F and no hotter. Brush with reserved marinade two or three times during smoking.

3. Fish is done when the flesh just flakes or the internal temperature is 130° F (1 to 2 hours of cooking time, depending on the thickness of the fish). Remove fish from smoker and serve hot or cold.

Serves 6.

Marinades In a small bowl, combine all ingredients and mix well with a whisk or fork. Keep track of the success of your recipes and adjust marinade ingredients to taste in future attempts.

Makes 1 cup.

COOKING CHART FOR WATER SMOKERS

	Weight or Thickness	Charcoal	Cooking Time*	Number of Wood Chunks	Types of Wood**	Internal Temperature When Done***
BEEF						
Boneless roasts	3–6 pounds	2 layers	4–6 hours	4–6	H, M, C, O, GV	125° F rare 140° F medium
Brisket of beef	6–8 pounds	2 layers	5–7 hours	5–8	H, M, C, O, GV	160°–170° F well
Short ribs	2–3 inches	2 layers	3–4 hours	4–6	H, M, C, O, GV	160°–170° F well
Prime rib bones	½ inch each	1 layer	2–3 hours	3–5	H, M, C, O, GV	140° F medium
LAMB AND GAME						
Leg of lamb	5–7 pounds	2 layers	4–6 hours	4–6	H, C, O, AP	140°–160° F medium
Venison roast	5–7 pounds	2 layers	4–6 hours	4–6	H, C, O, AP	160°–170° F well
Lamb shanks	1 pound each	2 layers	3–4 hours	4–6	H, C, O, AP	160°–170° F well
Lamb chops	1–1½ inches thick	1 layer	2–3 hours	4–6	H, C, O, AP	130°–140° F medium
PORK						
Boneless pork butt	4–6 pounds	2 layers	4–6 hours	5–8	H, AP, C, AL, GV, M	160°–170° F well
Boneless pork loin	3–5 pounds	2 layers	3–5 hours	4–6	H, AP, C, AL, GV, M	150°–160° F juicy, well
Fresh leg	12–18 pounds	2 layers	8–12 hours	7–10	H, AP, C, AL, GV, M	160°–170° F well
Pork chops	1¼ inches	2 layers	2–3 hours	4–6	H, AP, C, AL, GV, M	150°–160° F well
Ribs	Full slab	2 layers	3–5 hours	4–6	H, AP, C, AL, GV, M	160°–170° F well
Ham (cooked)	10–14 pounds	2 layers	3–4 hours	2–4	H, AP, C, AL, GV, M	130° F
Pork sausage (raw)	1 inch thick, such as Italian	1 layer	1½–2½ hours	2–4	H, AP, C, AL, GV, M	150°–160° F juicy
POULTRY						
Chicken	Cut up	1 layer	3–4 hours	2–4	AP, AL, C, GV, M, H, O	160°–170° F juicy
	3½–4½ pounds	2 layers	4–5 hours	3–5	AP, AL, C, GV, M, H, O	160°–170° F juicy
	5 pounds	2 layers	5–6 hours	4–6	AP, AL, C, GV, M, H, O	155°–165° F juicy
Turkey (unstuffed)	8–12 pounds	2 layers	7–8 hours	6–8	AP, AL, C, GV, M, H, O	160°–170° F juicy
	13–18 pounds	2 layers	9–12 hours	7–10	AP, AL, C, GV, M, H, O	160°–170° F juicy
Duck	4–6 pounds	2 layers	4–6 hours	3–5	AP, AL, C, GV, M, H, O	155°–165° F juicy
Cornish game hen	1–1½ pounds	1 layer	2–4 hours	2–4	AP, AL, C, GV, M, H, O	160°–170° F
Small birds	¾–1½ pounds	1 layer	2–4 hours	2–4	AP, AL, C, GV, M, H, O	160°–170° F
Pheasant	2–3 pounds	2 layers	3–5 hours	3–5	AP, AL, C, GV, M, H, O	160°–170° F
FISH						
Whole, small	¾–1½ pounds	½ layer	¾–1½ hours	2–4	AL, GV, O, M, H	Flakes
Whole, large	3–6 pounds	1 layer	3–4 hours	4–6	AL, GV, O, M, H	Flakes
Steak, fillet	1–1½ inches thick	1 layer	1–2½ hours	2–4	AL, GV, O, M, H	Flakes
Shellfish		1 layer	½–1½ hours	2–4	AL, GV, O, M, H	Firm to touch
VEGETABLES						
Winter squash (butternut, banana, acorn)	¾–1 inch	2 layers	2–3 hours	2–4	H, AP, C	Knife inserts easily
Summer squash (zucchini, crookneck, pattypan, golden zucchini)	Medium size	2 layers	1–2 hours	2–4	H, AP, C, M	Tender and soft
Onion	Medium	2 layers	2½–3½ hours	2–4	H, AP, C, M	Soft
Bell pepper	Medium	2 layers	¾–1½ hours	2–4	H, AP, C, M	Soft
Tomato	Medium	2 layers	½–¾ hours	2–4	H, AP, C, M	Soft
Corn	Whole	2 layers	½–¾ hours	2–4	H, AP, C, M	Tender
Garlic	Whole head	2 layers	2–3 hours	2–4	H, AP, C, M	Soft
Eggplant	¾-inch slices	2 layers	1½–2½ hours	2–4	H, AP, C, M	Soft

*The cooking times used in this chart are for meat that has been completely thawed. If frozen foods are used they should be completely defrosted. Always allow an extra 30 minutes of cooking—it is better to allow too much time rather than too little time. Foods can be kept hot beyond recommended time as long as the water pan is more than half full.

**AL=Alder, AP=Apple, C=Cherry, GV=Grapevine, H=Hickory, M=Mesquite, O=Oak.

***Insert instant-read thermometer into thickest part of meat or poultry. It should not touch bone.

SMOKED LAMB SHANKS WITH ROSEMARY MARINADE

Lamb shanks are a perfect choice for the water smoker. They are tough and need long, moist cooking to become juicy and tender. If you desire a saltier flavor, you can substitute the marinade described with the Lamb and Venison Brine (see page 52). Serve the shanks with basmati rice and a vegetable dish, such as Ratatouille of Smoked Summer Vegetables (see page 63), or use them in Smoked Lamb Shanks With Lentils (see page 67).

6 large lamb shanks (4 to 6 lb)
6 to 8 six-inch sprigs
*   *fresh rosemary*

Rosemary Marinade

½ cup red wine vinegar
¾ cup olive oil
4 cloves garlic, minced
2 tablespoons Dijon mustard
2 tablespoons fresh rosemary, chopped or 1 tablespoon dried rosemary
2 teaspoons each salt and pepper

1. Prepare Rosemary Marinade. Place lamb shanks in a large non-aluminum container and cover with marinade. Refrigerate, covered, 12 to 15 hours.

2. Prepare water smoker for smoke cooking (see page 49). Remove meat from marinade and reserve marinade. Add all but ½ cup reserved marinade to water pan, and then add water to fill pan. Place lamb on the grill. Cover and smoke between 200° F and 250° F. Add charcoal briquettes, wood, and water as needed. Baste with marinade every 2 hours. After 3 hours of cooking, check the temperature of the meat. When the lamb is at about 150° F, add rosemary branches to the coals. The lamb is done when the internal temperature of meat is between 155° F and 165° F, (3 to 4 hours of cooking time). Remove shanks from the smoker and serve immediately.

Serves 6.

Rosemary Marinade In a small bowl combine vinegar, olive oil, garlic, mustard, rosemary, salt, and pepper. Beat with a whisk until well mixed.

Makes 1¾ cups.

SMOKED PORK CHOPS IN SPICY BRINE

These pork chops are not nearly as salty as the prepared kind you buy in the store. The chops can be made up ahead of time, refrigerated, and cooked the next day with cabbage and sauerkraut (see page 67) or you can pan fry the chops briefly and accompany them with oven-baked yams. Smoked Pork Chops in Spicy Brine are shown in the photograph on page 53.

6 thick-cut (1¼ to 1½ in.) center cut pork chops (about 3 lb)
1 recipe Spicy Brine for Beef, Lamb, Pork, or Veal (see page 52)

1. Place meat in a non-aluminum container; cover with brine. Weight with a plate so that meat is completely immersed. Cure pork chops for 2 hours at room temperature or refrigerated overnight. Cure in the refrigerator for not more than 14 hours. Remove chops from brine, wash, and pat dry. Reserve brine.

2. Prepare water smoker for smoke cooking (see page 49). Fill water pan with a mixture of brine and water. Place chops on grill. Cover and smoke cook at 200° F to 250° F. Chops are done when the internal temperature of meat measures 150° F to 160° F (2 to 3 hours of cooking time). Serve immediately.

Serves 4.

SMOKED PORK BUTT WITH SAUTÉED APPLES

A combination born in paradise is smoked pork and sautéed apples. Instead of drinking wine with this meal, try a sparkling dry cider such as the type that comes from Normandy, France. Serve with home-fried potatoes and butter-glazed carrots.

1 Boston pork butt (5 to 6 lb)
1 recipe Aromatic Brine for Pork, Duck, or Chicken (see page 52)
4 cups sweet cider
3 green apples, halved, cored, and sliced
4 tablespoons butter
2 teaspoons sugar
2 tablespoons lemon juice
*   Pinch each ground cinnamon and ground nutmeg*

1. Place meat in a non-aluminum container and cover with brine. Weight pork with a plate so that it is completely immersed. Let cure in refrigerator for 2 days. It is not necessary for the cure to penetrate all the way to the center of the meat since the meat will be smoke cooked.

2. Prepare water smoker for smoke cooking (see page 49). Use 2 layers of charcoal briquettes and 3 to 5 chunks of wood. Add water to the smoker pan along with all but 1 cup of the cider. Remove pork from brine, wash, and pat dry.

3. Place meat on grill, fat side up. Cover and smoke cook at a temperature between 200° F and 250° F. Pork is done when the internal temperature is between 160° F and 170° F (after about 5 hours).

4. Remove meat to a cutting board and let rest while you prepare apples. In a 12-inch skillet over medium heat, melt butter. Add apples and fry on one side for 2 minutes. Turn apples and add sugar, lemon juice, remaining cider, cinnamon, and nutmeg. Cook 2 minutes more and remove pan from heat. Slice pork butt and place meat on a platter. Cover with sautéed apples and sauce. Serve immediately.

Serves 6 to 8.

SMOKED SHELLFISH

The following instructions should be considered guidelines—not rules—for preparing a variety of tasty combinations; let your imagination go. Combine different types of shellfish and prepare them in a brine and one of two marinades, or make one batch in each marinade. To prevent the shellfish from falling through the grill of the water smoker, place a piece of mesh screen over the grill or use aluminum foil with several small holes punched into it. Once smoked, the brined shellfish is better cold than hot. The marinated shellfish is good hot or cold. Well-wrapped smoked shellfish will keep 3 to 5 days refrigerated. It does not freeze well.

Brine Method

2 pounds raw shellfish such as shucked oysters, mussels, scallops, or unshelled raw shrimp
1 recipe Fish Brine (see page 52)
1 cup oil

1. Place shellfish in a large non-aluminum container. Cover with Fish Brine and let soak at room temperature 30 to 45 minutes. Remove shellfish, wash, and pat dry. Brush with half the oil.

2. Prepare water smoker for smoke cooking (see page 49). Do not use water pan. Cover and smoke cook at 170° F to 210° F. Use 20 to 30 briquettes and 4 cups soaked wood chips or 2 to 4 wood chunks. Shellfish is done when it is firm and opaque. If you can measure the internal temperature of seafood, it should register about 120° F. Smoking time is between 45 minutes and 1½ hours. Do not overcook. Remove from grill and brush with remaining oil. Refrigerate until chilled. Serve cold.

Marinade Method

2 pounds raw shellfish such as shucked oysters, mussels, scallops, or unshelled raw shrimp
1 recipe Lime-Ginger Marinade or Lemon and Fresh Herb Marinade (see page 58)

1. Place shellfish in a large non-aluminum container. Cover with marinade and let rest at room temperature for 30 minutes. Do not marinate too long or the acid in the marinade will begin to "cook" the seafood. Remove shellfish from marinade and reserve marinade.

2. Prepare water smoker for smoke cooking (see page 49). Do not use water pan. Cover and smoke cook at 170° F to 210° F. Use about 20 to 30 briquettes and 4 cups soaked wood chips or 2 to 4 wood chunks. Brush seafood once or twice with marinade during smoking. Shellfish is done when firm and opaque. If you can measure the internal temperature of seafood, it should register about 120° F. Smoking time is between 45 minutes and 1½ hours. Do not overcook. Remove from grill and brush with remaining marinade. Serve hot or cold.

Serves 4 to 6.

A two-day curing time and five hours in the water smoker means that serving Smoked Pork Butt With Sautéed Apples (opposite page) will take some planning, although little actual hands-on work. Each stage takes just a few minutes and the tasty combination of spicy meat with fresh apples that sings of autumn will be worthy of your efforts. Serve with sparkling dry cider.

Ratatouille is a traditional vegetarian dish of Provence, France. This smoked version may be served as a side dish, entrée, or an hors d'oeuvre.

RATATOUILLE OF SMOKED SUMMER VEGETABLES

Summer is filled with the bounty of fresh and full-flavored vegetables. Ratatouille is a great dish that takes advantage of this abundance. This vegetable ragout is usually stewed indoors, but the use of the water smoker to cook the vegetables adds a whole new dimension and a subtle smoky flavor to the dish. The different vegetables need different amounts of time to cook, so add them to the water smoker in stages. Total cooking time is about 3½ hours. Finish cooking the ratatouille over the stove to allow all flavors to intermingle and to continue cooking vegetables, which were not completely done. Ratatouille is best eaten warm or at room temperature.

> 2 *medium onions*
> 1 *cup olive oil*
> 2 *whole heads garlic*
> 3 *small zucchini, cut lengthwise in half*
> 3 *crookneck squash, cut lengthwise in half*
> 1 *medium eggplant, cut into ¾-inch-thick slices*
> 6 *medium tomatoes*
> 1 *red bell pepper, cut into 8 wedges*
> 1 *yellow bell pepper, cut into 8 wedges*
> 1 *green bell pepper, cut into 8 wedges*
> ¼ *cup coarsely chopped fresh basil*
> 2 *tablespoons lemon juice*
> ½ *teaspoon ground coriander*
> *Salt and pepper, to taste*
> ½ *cup chopped parsley, for garnish*

1. Prepare water smoker for smoke cooking (see page 49). Vegetables will smoke cook at 220° F to 260° F for a total of 2½ to 3½ hours. Add charcoal briquettes, wood, and water as needed.

2. Remove most of the outer skins of onions. Cut several vertical slashes into each and brush with olive oil. Place on grill and smoke cook for 2½ to 3½ hours.

3. Using a small paring knife, cut through the outer layers of skin on each garlic head; remove skin. Brush with olive oil, place on grill, and smoke cook for 2 to 3 hours.

4. After 1 to 2 hours, brush zucchini, squash, and eggplant slices with olive oil and arrange on the grill. Smoke cook for 1 to 1½ hours.

5. Brush tomatoes and bell peppers with olive oil and add to grill. Smoke cook these for 30 to 45 minutes. Remove other vegetables form the grill if they are soft.

6. At end of smoking time, remove all vegetables from the grill. Cut away darkened outer skins and slice onions. Squeeze garlic cloves (discard skins), chop tomatoes, and transfer all vegetables to a large mixing bowl.

7. Add remaining olive oil, basil, lemon juice, coriander, and salt and pepper to vegetables in the mixing bowl. Gently toss. Transfer mixture to a large pot or Dutch oven. Cover and simmer on stove until all vegetables are completely cooked and the flavors have mingled (20 to 30 minutes). Transfer to a shallow bowl or platter. Garnish with chopped parsley and serve.

Serves 6 to 8.

SMOKED WINTER SQUASH WITH MAPLE SYRUP

The water smoker performs very well for cooking vegetables. The moist heat steams the vegetables while they develop a mild smoky flavor. Firm vegetables such as winter squash are well suited for this type of cooking. The squash goes well with pork roast, pork chops, turkey, or duck. Smoke the vegetable at the same time you cook your main course, or smoke the vegetable in advance, refrigerate, and bake in maple syrup up to five days later. This dish is shown in the photograph on page 53.

> *Salt and pepper, to taste*
> 4 *to 6 pounds acorn, butternut, or yellow winter squash, each cut into 4 to 6 wedges with seeds removed*
> *Oil, for brushing*
> ½ *cup maple syrup*
> ½ *cup butter, plus butter for pan*
> *Pinch each ground nutmeg and ground cinnamon*

1. Prepare water smoker for smoke cooking (see page 49). Lightly sprinkle salt and pepper on squash. Brush with oil and arrange on water smoker grill with cut side down. Smoke cook at 200° F to 240° F until squash is tender when knife is inserted (2 to 3 hours). Remove from grill. Squash can be refrigerated at this point and preparation completed up to 5 days later.

2. Preheat oven to 350° F. With a paring knife remove skin from squash and cut into 2-inch chunks. Butter a 9- by 12-inch baking dish and add squash. Pour maple syrup over squash and scatter pats of butter over top. Sprinkle lightly with nutmeg and cinnamon. Cover with aluminum foil and bake for 15 minutes. Remove foil and gently stir squash to coat with butter, syrup, and spices. Continue to bake, uncovered, for an additional 30 minutes. Serve directly from baking dish or transfer to serving dish.

Serves 8 to 10.

SMOKED COUNTRY SAUSAGE

Making sausage is not difficult, and the results are rewarding. You will probably find that even your first attempts at homemade sausage taste better than most storebought varieties. This is a basic recipe that allows you to use your own imagination. You may want to add cold wine instead of ice water and use other seasonings, such as fresh thyme, basil, or other herbs. You can mix in venison, beef, veal, or lamb with the pork, but don't leave the pork fat out of the recipe. In addition, the sausage must be cased in something. Traditionally, dried and salted animal intestines called casings are used for this purpose. Casings come packed in salt and may be purchased from a butcher-supply store or by mail order (see page 121). If you do not have the equipment for stuffing casings, use cheesecloth and string instead. This recipe includes a detailed description of stuffing and linking sausage that should make the process clear to a beginner. Smoke-cooked sausage will keep refrigerated for five to seven days; frozen sausages will keep up to three months. Do not store these sausages at room temperature since they do not contain the bacterial retardant sodium nitrite.

2¼ pounds lean pork butt, cut into 1-inch pieces

¾ pound pork fat, cut into 1-inch pieces

1 tablespoon salt

2 teaspoons minced garlic

2 teaspoons paprika

1 teaspoon cayenne pepper

½ teaspoon each *dried sage and dried summer savory*

2 teaspoons sugar

½ cup ice water

6 to 8 feet medium hog casing or 2 feet cheesecloth and some string

1. Chill pieces of meat and fat in the freezer for 30 minutes. In a food processor or meat grinder fitted with a ⅜-inch plate, grind all meat and fat. If using a food processor, grind in small batches of a little less than ½ pound each. Chop coarsely, yielding ⅜-inch dice. In a 12- to 14-inch mixing bowl, combine meat, fat, salt, garlic, paprika, cayenne, sage, savory, sugar, and the ice water. Mix well with your hands, kneading and squeezing as you mix. Do not overmix because fat will begin to melt.

2. Make a small sample to check seasoning: Heat a small skillet over medium heat. Make one small patty of meat mixture and fry 5 minutes; turn and fry 3 more minutes. Taste patty and correct seasonings in remaining raw mixture.

3. *If using cheesecloth:* If you are not stuffing sausage mixture into casings, shape mixture into 6 cylinders, each 8 to 10 inches long and 1½ to 2 inches in diameter. Wrap tightly in 2 layers of cheesecloth and tie each end with string. Proceed with step 5.

If using hog casing: Remove a length of casing from the salt it is shipped in and place in a bowl of warm water. Place bowl in the sink and hold one end of casing up to the kitchen faucet. Gently run warm water through casing to wash out salt. Continue to soak casing in warm water for 1 hour, or until casing is soft and slippery. Attach the sausage-stuffing horn to the front of the meat grinder. Don't forget to remove the plate and knife. Find one end of the casing, spread it open, and scoop a little of water from the bowl into casing. The water will help to lubricate as you gently pull all the casing onto the horn. Let the last 3 to 4 inches dangle in front of the horn. Fill grinder with sausage mixture and feed mixture through grinder until it begins to enter the casing. Tie the end into a knot, and prick any air bubbles that appear. (Two pairs of hands are helpful in the stuffing process.) Continue to stuff casing, gently holding onto the horn with your thumb to control the rate and tightness of the filling. Do not fill

too full, or sausages will burst during linking and smoking. With casing still attached to horn, remove horn from grinder and push any remaining mixture through it with the handle of a wooden spoon. Cut the end of the casing 3 inches beyond the meat, and tie into a knot. Drain any casing that you did not use; resalt it and refrigerate.

4. To link: Pinch sausage at 4- to 6-inch intervals, and twist three to four complete turns. Pinch off again and once again so that you end up twisting every other link. Alternate the direction you twist each time. There should be ½ to 1 inch of twisted casing between each link. Cut each link in the middle of each twist, thereby sealing the ends of each. If sausage bursts (and this happens to the best of cooks), either restuff or use the mixture in patty form.

5. Once in the casings, the meats, spices, and other flavoring need time to mature. Maturation contributes to a mellow flavor. Place sausage uncovered on a rack in the refrigerator, or suspend them by hooking to a rack in the refrigerator. Let sausages rest overnight.

6. The next day prepare water smoker for smoke cooking (see page 49). Place links on grill. Cover and smoke cook at 170° F to 200° F. Add charcoal briquettes, wood, and water as needed. The sausage is done when the internal temperature of meat is 150° F to 160° F (1½ to 2½ hours of cooking). Remove sausage from smoker and serve immediately, or refrigerate for later use.

Makes 3 pounds sausage.

Note To reheat sausage: Place links in skillet with ¼ inch water. Cover and cook over medium heat for 10 to 15 minutes, turning occasionally.

PASTRAMI

Transplanted New Yorkers take heart: With very little trouble you can make your own pastrami! For this method of smoking, you don't need to include the nitrite in the cure. The pastrami will have a gray appearance, but the color will not affect the flavor.

- 1 to 2 recipes Corned Beef or Pastrami Brine (see page 53)
- 2 trimmed beef briskets (6 to 8 lb each) or 4 beef plates (3 to 4 lb each)
- 2 cups cracked coriander seed
- 1 cup cracked peppercorns

1. Place meat in a non-aluminum container and cover with brine. Weight down meat with a heavy plate so that it stays submerged. Place container in refrigerator and cure for 4 days. At this point overhaul brine (see page 52). Continue to cure for 3 to 4 more days or until cure has penetrated to the center of meat. Remove meat, wash, and drain. Combine coriander and pepper and rub all over meat.

2. Prepare water smoker for smoke cooking (see page 49). Use only 30 briquettes to begin so that the temperature in the smoker does not exceed 200° F. Use 5 to 8 wood chunks or 1½ quarts soaked wood chips. Place meat on both racks of smoker, cover, and smoke cook until internal temperature of meat is 120° F to 130° F (3 to 4 hours of cooking).

3. Add enough briquettes (about 40) and 2 or 3 chunks of wood or 3 cups wood chips to the fire to build up the temperature in the smoker to between 220° F and 250° F. Continue to smoke cook until the internal temperature of meat is 160° F to 165° F (another 3 to 4 hours of cooking). Remove meat and let rest 10 minutes before slicing. Refrigerate leftovers.

Each brisket makes enough for 15 sandwiches; each plate makes enough for 10 sandwiches.

Note To reheat whole pastrami for sandwiches: Allow pastrami to cool overnight in the refrigerator. The next day place pastrami in a Dutch oven with about 1 inch water, 1 whole head garlic, and 2 tablespoons pickling spice. Cover pot and simmer for 1 to 1½ hours, or until meat is tender when a fork or knife is inserted. Remove meat from pot and let rest for 10 minutes. Slice thin for sandwiches.

Note To reheat leftover pastrami: Cut thin slices and place on a vegetable steamer in a pot with 1 to 2 inches water in the bottom. Cover pot and steam for 1 to 2 minutes.

There is no need to rush out to a delicatessen during halftime when you have your own smoked meats such as Pastrami and Smoked Country Sausage (opposite page) on hand at home. Just remember to pick up chips, pickles, sandwich fixings, and plenty of beer before the game begins.

Smoked Lamb Shanks With Lentils (opposite page) is easy on pocketbook and cook. The meat, vegetables, and beans provide a balanced meal in one dish.

USING SMOKED FOOD

Including smoked foods in salads and side dishes adds a flavorful dimension to any meal. The recipes in this section highlight the cold smoked classics and the smoke-cooked foods prepared in the water smoker, but you can use storebought smoked foods for these dishes as well.

SMOKED SALMON PIE

You can substitute trout, whitefish, or sturgeon for the salmon in this recipe. Prepare the pie shell a day ahead to reduce the preparation time. The dish can be served as an appetizer or as a simple lunch or supper. Lonnie Gandara wrote this recipe, which originally appeared in the California Culinary Academy series cookbook *Fish & Shellfish*.

2 *tablespoons unsalted butter*
¾ *cup chopped green onion*
6 *ounces Smoked Salmon (see page 54), chopped Kosher salt and freshly ground black pepper, to taste Dash cayenne pepper, or to taste*
½ *pound ricotta cheese*
2 *large eggs, lightly beaten 9-inch pastry shell, baked*

1. Preheat oven to 350° F. In a medium skillet melt butter. Add onion and sauté until soft. Stir in salmon, salt and pepper, and cayenne.

2. Mix cheese with beaten eggs, then pour into pie shell. Spoon salmon mixture over cheese mixture and spread evenly.

3. Bake until set, 45 to 50 minutes. Let rest 5 minutes before serving.

Serves 6 to 8.

SMOKED LAMB SHANKS WITH LENTILS

This hearty and inexpensive dish provides a substantial and balanced meal. You only need to make a salad or steamed vegetable to serve with it. You can leave the meat on the shank bones, but by removing it you can feed more people. If there are leftovers, grease a casserole with olive oil, add leftover lentils, brush top with more olive oil, and sprinkle with bread crumbs. Bake uncovered at 350° F for 45 minutes.

1 *recipe Smoked Lamb Shank With Rosemary Marinade (see page 60), remove meat from 4 shanks and reserve lamb and bones*
4 *cups beef or chicken stock or water*
½ *teaspoon each ground cumin and ground oregano*
1 *teaspoon each paprika and pepper*
¼ *teaspoon cayenne pepper*
½ *teaspoon ground coriander*
2 *bay leaves*
¼ *teaspoon dried thyme*
½ *teaspoon dried basil*
3 *cloves garlic, minced*
2 *cups dried lentils*
1 *onion, coarsely chopped*
1 *carrot, coarsely chopped*
1 *rib celery, coarsely chopped Salt, to taste*

1. In a 4-quart Dutch oven, cover shank bones with stock. Add cumin, oregano, paprika, pepper, cayenne, coriander, bay leaves, thyme, basil, and garlic. Bring to a boil. Reduce heat, cover, and simmer for 30 to 45 minutes.

2. Add lentils, onion, carrot, celery, and meat, making sure they are completely covered by liquid. Add more liquid if needed. Cover pot and continue to simmer until lentils are soft but still whole (about 45 minutes). Salt to taste. Drain any liquid and discard bones. Transfer to a shallow bowl and serve.

Serves 4 to 6.

SMOKED PORK CHOPS BRAISED WITH CABBAGE AND SAUERKRAUT

This quick and simple version of the Alsatian classic *choucroute garni* can be made with your own home-smoked pork chops (see page 60) or with storebought smoked chops. In addition to the pork chops, you can add 1½ pounds of sausage. Use your own home-smoked sausages or storebought varieties such as knockwurst, bratwürst, garlic sausage, or frankfurters. Serve with boiled new potatoes and lots of mustard.

¼ *pound bacon, diced*
1 *onion, sliced*
1 *carrot, diced*
½ *cabbage, quartered and thinly sliced*
1 *pound sauerkraut, drained*
½ *cup beef stock*
1 *cup beer*
1 *teaspoon caraway seed*
4 *bay leaves*
2 *teaspoons pepper*
1 *recipe Smoked Pork Chops in Spicy Brine (see page 60)*
1½ *pounds Smoked Country Sausage (see page 64), optional*

In a heavy Dutch oven over medium heat, fry bacon until crisp. Add onion and carrot. Cover and cook 5 minutes, stirring occasionally. Add cabbage, cover, and cook another 5 minutes, stirring frequently until cabbage is wilted. Add sauerkraut, beef stock, beer, caraway, bay leaves, and pepper. Bring to a boil, then reduce heat to simmer. Cook covered for at least 1 hour. Add pork chops and sausages, if used. Gently braise for an additional 20 to 30 minutes. Serve hot.

Serves 6.

SMOKED CHICKEN SALAD

Smoked chicken makes a wonderful chicken salad. Make sure to add about ¼ cup of finely shredded skin, which has most of the smoky flavor, to the salad. Use the chicken salad for sandwiches or as a cold salad plate at lunch.

> 3 to 4 cups cooked Smoked Chicken (see page 56), cut into 1-inch dice
> ¼ cup shredded smoked chicken skin
> 1 tablespoon lemon juice
> 1 cup mayonnaise
> 2 teaspoons capers
> 1 tablespoon chopped parsley
> 1 tablespoon chopped green onion
> Salt and pepper, to taste
> 4 large lettuce leaves (optional) Lemon wedges, for garnish

In a medium mixing bowl, toss chicken and skin with lemon juice. Add mayonnaise, capers, parsley, green onion, and salt and pepper. Stir until chicken is well coated with mayonnaise. If serving as a salad, place a lettuce leaf on each plate and mound with one quarter of the salad. Garnish with lemon wedges and serve.

Serves 4 as a salad or makes 3 or 4 generous sandwiches.

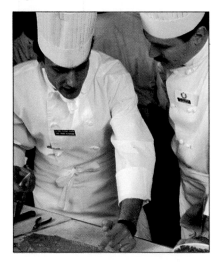

SMOKED CHICKEN AND FRESH APRICOT SALAD

Try this wonderful variation of the Smoked Chicken Salad in the summer, when fresh apricots are available. Other times of the year you can use canned apricots or frozen apricot purée.

> 8 dried apricots
> 4 ripe, fresh apricots, pitted or 3 canned apricots, pitted or ⅓ cup apricot purée and eliminate lemon juice
> 1 tablespoon lemon juice
> ¾ cup mayonnaise
> 1 tablespoon chopped parsley
> ¼ cup shredded smoked chicken skin (see page 56)
> 3 to 4 cups cooked smoked chicken meat (see page 56), cut into 1-inch dice
> Salt and ground pepper, to taste
> 8 fresh or canned apricots, halved and pitted, for garnish

1. In a small saucepan cover dried apricots with water and bring to a boil. Cover and simmer for 10 minutes. Drain and cool under cold, running water. Chop coarsely and set aside.

2. In a food processor or blender combine fresh apricots and lemon juice; purée. (This step is not necessary if using prepared apricot purée.)

3. In a large mixing bowl, combine mayonnaise, parsley, chicken skin, and chicken meat. Add apricot purée and dried apricots and mix until chicken is well coated. Salt and pepper to taste. Chill. Serve on small individual plates garnished with fresh apricot halves.

Serves 4.

SMOKED FISH SALAD WITH LEMON-DILL DRESSING

This salad makes a superb summertime picnic dish, or serve it as an appetizer or a luncheon dish in the cool months. Any white-fleshed smoked fish works well in this recipe; use trout, whitefish, sturgeon, cod, or leftover smoked fish steaks or fillets.

> 1½ pounds small red potatoes, quartered
> 2 tablespoons wine vinegar
> 1 pound smoked fish (such as Smoked Trout, page 56, or Smoked Fish Fillet, page 58), all bones removed
> ¼ cup chopped red onion
> ½ cup green onion, finely chopped
> 1 cup parsley, finely chopped

Lemon-Dill Dressing

> 2 teaspoons Dijon mustard
> 1 tablespoon wine vinegar
> 4 tablespoons lemon juice
> 1 teaspoon each salt and pepper
> ½ cup olive oil
> 1 tablespoon fresh dill

1. Boil potatoes in salted water until a knife inserts easily (about 20 minutes). Drain and briefly toss with vinegar. Cover and refrigerate until cool (about 20 minutes).

2. Using your hands, break fish into small bite-sized pieces. Combine potatoes, all but ¼ cup of fish, red and green onions, and parsley. Add dressing and toss only enough to distribute ingredients evenly; tossing too much causes potatoes to fall apart. Place salad in shallow bowl or serving platter. Arrange remaining fish on top and serve.

Serves 4 to 6.

Lemon-Dill Dressing In a small mixing bowl, combine mustard, vinegar, lemon juice, salt, and pepper. Gradually beat in olive oil to produce a creamy dressing. Stir in dill.

Makes 1 cup.

CHINESE SMOKED-DUCK SALAD

This recipe uses leftover Smoked Duck (see page 56) and is adapted from a recipe written by Cynthia Scheer for the California Culinary Academy series cookbook *Salads*. The puffy-crisp rice noodles (or sticks) that add so much appeal to this distinctive salad are sometimes labeled with their Chinese name, *mai fun*. Look for them in the foreign food section of your supermarket or in markets that specialize in Asian foods. To assure maximum volume and crispness, be sure the oil for frying is heated to the temperature specified.

2 tablespoons sesame seed
½ tablespoon each *Asian sesame oil and salad oil*
½ cup *Smoked Duck skin, shredded (see page 56)*
2 to 3 cups *Smoked Duck (see page 56), diced*
  Salt, to taste
  Oil, for frying
  Rice sticks
4 cups *shredded iceberg lettuce*
4 *green onions, thinly sliced*
½ cup *coarsely chopped cilantro*

Hoisin Dressing

2 tablespoons each *hoisin sauce and lemon juice*
2 *teaspoons sugar*
1 *tablespoon Asian sesame oil*
3 *tablespoons salad oil (preferably peanut)*

1. Prepare Hoisin dressing. Then, in a small skillet over medium heat, stir sesame seed until lightly browned (6 to 8 minutes). Remove from skillet and set aside.

2. Pour sesame oil and salad oil in a wok or large skillet; turn heat to medium high. Stir-fry duck skin, stirring and turning until it is crispy (about 5 minutes). Add duck meat and cook for 2 minutes more. Salt to taste.

3. Mix duck with Hoisin Dressing and let rest while assembling salad.

4. To fry rice sticks: Pour oil for frying into a wok or large, deep skillet to a depth of about 2 inches; heat to 350° F. Add a generous handful of rice sticks. Stir and fry just until puffy and crisp, 15 to 30 seconds. Remove from oil and drain well. You should have about 2 cups.

5. In a large bowl or deep platter, mix lettuce, green onion, and cilantro. Add duck with dressing, sesame seed, and rice sticks and mix lightly. Serve at once.

Serves 4.

Hoisin Dressing In a small bowl mix hoisin sauce, lemon juice, and sugar. Using a whisk or fork, gradually beat in sesame oil and salad oil.

Makes about ½ cup.

This luncheon version of Smoked Fish Salad With Lemon-Dill Dressing (opposite page) features Smoked Trout (see page 56). If you're planning this dish for a picnic, pack the salad and the dressing separately and wait until just before serving to toss them together.

THANKSGIVING
SMOKED TURKEY DINNER

Cranberry, Brandy, Apricot Sauce

Baked Oysters in the Half Shell

*Smoked Turkey With
Soy-Ginger Marinade*

*Italian Sausage and
Fresh Fennel Stuffing*

Down-Home Mashed Potatoes

American-Style Turkey Gravy

*Stuffed Baked Yams
With Bourbon Butter*

Green Beans With Tasso Butter

Pecan Pie

*Beverage Suggestions: Sparkling
Wine and Cranberry-Apple Juice*

---

*While the turkey slowly cooks
in the water smoker, your
inside ovens are free to cook
the rest of the dishes on the
menu to the finishing point.
When the turkey is done, it
can sit on the water smoker
for an hour or rest on the
carving board for 40
minutes—just enough time
to finish up the yams and
stuffing. All recipes serve
8, with plenty of leftovers.*

PREPARATION PLAN

Smoked turkey is just as delicious cold as hot, and if your guests or family do not insist on hot turkey, you can cook the bird a day ahead. (Rewarming this turkey is not recommended, however.) Whether you eat the turkey hot or cold on Thanksgiving Day, make sure there are plenty of leftovers to make a Dagwood Sandwich (see page 75). Save the carcass to make a hearty soup. Because the flavor is hamlike, it will make a fine base for split-pea, lentil, or bean soup. Smoked turkey needs no gravy, but if you want to pour gravy over your stuffing and potatoes, follow the simple gravy recipe provided. Do not stuff this turkey; Italian Sausage and Fresh Fennel Stuffing is excellent cooked in a casserole. If you wish to use this stuffing to stuff a turkey that will be cooked in a regular oven, use about one cup less liquid since the stuffing will pick up juices from the turkey.

CRANBERRY, BRANDY, APRICOT SAUCE

Feel free to make this sauce ahead of the holiday rush as it will keep refrigerated for 2 to 3 weeks. It is extremely easy to make and so much more interesting than the tiresome canned variety.

- 2 *cups* each *water and sugar*
- 2 *pounds fresh cranberries*
- 1 *cup apricot preserves*
- ½ *cup* each *lemon juice and brandy*

In a 4- to 6-quart heavy pot, boil the water with sugar until sugar is dissolved. Add cranberries. Bring to a boil and lower heat to a simmer. Cook until cranberries begin to burst (about 20 minutes). Add preserves, lemon juice, and brandy. Cook an additional 5 minutes. Cool and store in refrigerator until ready for use. This sauce will keep refrigerated for 2 to 3 weeks.

Makes 6 to 8 cups.

BAKED OYSTERS
IN THE HALF SHELL

This recipe was adapted from a recipe for barbecued oysters written by Jay Harlow that appeared in the California Culinary Academy series cookbook *Regional American Classics*. If you are adept at opening raw oysters, shuck them first, add the butter sauce, and bake for 10 minutes. If you're not, the oysters will open on their own—just follow this recipe and wait and see.

- ½ *cup butter, softened*
- 4 *cloves garlic, minced or pressed*
  Juice and grated peel of ½ lemon
- ½ *teaspoon freshly ground pepper*
- 3 *dozen small or medium oysters, in the shell*

1. One day ahead: In a medium bowl combine butter, garlic, lemon peel and juice, and pepper; beat until light and thoroughly mixed. Form into a thin log on a sheet of waxed paper, wrap ends of paper around log securely by rolling log, and wrap tightly in plastic wrap. Refrigerate until 1 hour before using.

2. Preheat oven to 450° F. Place unopened oysters in a baking pan with the deep side of the shell down. As soon as oysters begin to open, remove them from the oven. Make sure you use an oven mitt or pot holder—they will be very hot. When oysters are cool enough to handle, remove top shells and cut each oyster from bottom shell. Discard top shells. Place a pat of about 1 teaspoon butter on each oyster and return oysters to oven. Serve as soon as juices are bubbly and butter is melted (about 5 minutes).

*Serves about 9 as first course
(4 oysters each).*

Smoked Turkey is the focal point of a traditional Thanksgiving menu that has a few innovative twists. Portions were planned to provide plenty of leftovers.

One reason for preparing *Smoked Turkey With Soy-Ginger Marinade is that the recipe employs a water smoker, leaving the kitchen oven available for cooking vegetables and pies. However, the main reason to make smoked turkey is because it tastes so good. The mahogany-colored skin covers moist, savory meat. Shown here is a typical home-style water smoker. If necessary, see page 78 for details on converting a gas grill to a water smoker.*

SMOKED TURKEY WITH SOY-GINGER MARINADE

Allow plenty of time for this bird to cook, especially the first time you attempt smoking a turkey. The temperature of the fire and even the outside air temperature will affect the cooking time. The skin of the finished turkey will be a rich mahogany color.

    1 turkey (12 to 14 lb)
    2 cups light soy sauce
    2 tablespoons minced
       fresh ginger
    2 teaspoons minced fresh garlic
    2 tablespoons sugar
    1 cup medium-dry sherry
    ¼ cup Asian sesame oil
    ½ cup rice vinegar or
       wine vinegar

1. Remove giblets and neck from turkey and save for gravy. Remove last two joints of each wing and save for gravy. Wash turkey thoroughly inside and out with cold running water, drain, and pat dry.

2. To make marinade: In a large stainless-steel bowl, combine soy sauce, ginger, garlic, sugar, sherry, sesame oil, and vinegar. Place turkey in bowl and rub marinade into cavity and on the outside of bird. Cover and refrigerate 1 to 2 days, turning turkey three or four times during that period.

3. Remove bird from marinade and reserve marinade. Follow directions for smoke cooking (see page 49). Add all but 1 cup of reserved marinade to water pan, then fill pan with hot water. Place turkey on grill, breast side up, cover and and smoke cook 7 to 9 hours at 200° F to 240° F. Add charcoal, wood, and water as needed.

4. After 6 hours insert an instant-read thermometer into thickest part of thigh. Turkey is done when thermometer reads 160° F to 170° F; remove thermometer and continue to smoke cook until this temperature is reached. Baste with reserved marinade two or three times during cooking. Serve turkey warm or cool. Wrap and refrigerate leftovers.

Serves 8 to 10 generously.

<u>Note</u> You can convert a gas grill to a water smoker in order to smoke a whole turkey. However, the flavor will be somewhat less intense. See page 78 for general instructions. It is possible to convert some brands of kettle-shaped grills into water smokers as well. Check manufacturer's instructions for details.

ITALIAN SAUSAGE AND FRESH FENNEL STUFFING

The better tasting the sausage is that you use for this dressing, the better your final result. Remember, you do not stuff this dressing into a turkey that will be smoked. It is designed to be cooked in a casserole inside an oven. If you want to adapt it for use inside a bird, only use 1 to 2 cups of stock because the dressing will pick up moisture from the turkey.

> 4 tablespoons butter, plus butter for baking dish
> 1½ pounds mild Italian fennel sausage, removed from casing
> 1 bulb fresh fennel
> 2 ribs celery, coarsely chopped
> 1 cup coarsely chopped onion
> 1 tablespoon minced garlic
> 1 teaspoon ground sage
> 8 to 10 cups cubed dried bread
> 2 to 3 cups turkey or chicken broth
> Salt and pepper, to taste

1. Preheat oven to 350° F. In the 4 tablespoons butter in a 12-inch skillet over medium heat, fry sausage for about 10 minutes, breaking meat into small pieces.

2. Cut off tough shoots from fennel and coarsely chop bulb into ½-inch pieces. Add fennel, celery, onion, garlic, and sage to sausage; cook covered until vegetables are soft (10 to 12 minutes). Place sausage and vegetable mixture in a large mixing bowl along with dried bread. Add 2 cups stock and mix well. Stuffing should be moist enough to just stick together when mounded on a spoon; add more stock if necessary. Season with salt and pepper.

3. Butter a 2- to 3-quart baking dish. Fill with stuffing and bake, covered, for 45 minutes.

Serves 8 to 10.

DOWN-HOME MASHED POTATOES

This recipe was written by Naomi Wise and Michael Goodwin and originally appeared in the California Culinary Academy cookbook *Regional American Classics*. Mashed potatoes need not be perfectly smooth; in fact, a few lumps improve the texture. Nor should the milk be premeasured and heated; the quantity needed depends on the type and age of the potatoes. (Potatoes that have been stored for a while take more milk than new potatoes.) Pour milk in gradually until the potatoes are the way you like them.

> 1 medium-large (about 11 oz) potato per person
> 1 tablespoon butter for each potato
> Milk as needed (¼ to ½ cup per potato)
> Salt and white pepper, to taste
> Paprika, for garnish

1. Bring a large pot of salted water to a boil. Meanwhile, peel potatoes and quarter or halve them (depending on size). Drop potato pieces into pot as they are peeled, even if water is not quite boiling. Cook potatoes over high heat until tender (about 25 minutes after water comes to a boil). Some pieces can be a little underdone. Drain well.

2. Place potatoes and butter in a large bowl. Using a potato masher or fork, coarsely mash them together. Make a well in the center and pour in a small amount of milk.

3. With an electric mixer (*not* a blender or food processor, which turn potatoes into a starchy goo) beat potatoes, adding more milk a little at a time as needed, until the desired texture is obtained. After tasting add salt and pepper. At this point potatoes can be set aside, uncovered, until the rest of dinner is nearly ready. Thirty minutes before serving time, preheat oven to 350° F.

4. Mound potatoes in an ovenproof casserole, sprinkle with paprika, and bake uncovered 20 minutes.

Serves 8 to 10.

AMERICAN-STYLE TURKEY GRAVY

This recipe is adapted from the California Culinary Academy series cookbook *Regional American Classics* and was originally written by Naomi Wise and Michael Goodwin. Using some of the liquid from the water pan of the smoker adds a subtle smoky flavor that complements the smoked turkey.

> Turkey neck, wing tips, and giblets, chopped
> 6 cups cold water
> 1 large onion, trimmed and quartered
> 1 carrot, coarsely chopped
> 1 stalk celery, coarsely chopped
> 4 tablespoons butter
> 6 tablespoons flour
> 2 cups liquid from the water pan in the smoker
> 1 cup heavy cream
> Salt, white pepper, and ground nutmeg, to taste
> Lemon juice, to taste (optional)

1. Place turkey neck, wing tips, and giblets in a heavy 2-quart saucepan. Cover with the water. Bring to a boil over high heat, and skim off scum from the top. Add onion, carrot, and celery and return to a boil. Lower heat to a simmer and cook slowly until liquid has reduced to a rich broth and volume has been reduced to 2 cups (about 2 hours). Strain and reserve.

2. Melt butter in a medium-sized heavy pan. Add flour and stir over low heat until flour begins to turn golden (about 2 minutes). Pour in turkey broth and liquid from water pan, stirring vigorously until smooth. Stirring constantly, bring mixture to a boil. Stir in cream. Lower heat and simmer about 5 minutes longer to thicken, stirring occasionally. Season with salt, white pepper, and nutmeg; add lemon juice by drops, if desired.

Makes about 5 cups.

STUFFED BAKED YAMS WITH BOURBON BUTTER

These yams are another great dish to serve for holiday entertaining as they can be prepared a day or two ahead, wrapped, stored in the refrigerator, and then baked in the oven for about half an hour right along with the mashed potatoes. These yams are also perfect as a main dish. Serve with a tossed green salad for a meal somewhat lighter than the traditional Thanksgiving meal.

    10 to 12 yams
     1 cup unsalted butter
     ½ cup firmly packed
        brown sugar
     ¼ cup bourbon
     ½ teaspoon salt
        Pinch each *ground nutmeg,
        ground cinnamon, and
        ground cardamom*

1. Preheat oven to 400° F. Wash yams and pat dry. Place yams on baking sheet, place in the middle of oven, and cook until yams are soft (45 minutes).

2. Remove yams from oven, let cool for 10 minutes, and cut yams open. Scoop out most of meat, taking care not to rip skins. In a medium bowl combine yam meat, butter, brown sugar, bourbon, salt, nutmeg, cinnamon, and cardamom. Mix with electric mixer until smooth. Stuff mixture into yam skins. The restuffed yams may be refrigerated at this point for up to 2 days and rewarmed later. Bake in a 350° F oven for 20 to 30 minutes. Serve immediately.

Serves 8 to 10.

GREEN BEANS WITH TASSO BUTTER

Tasso, a Cajun seasoning meat, is usually made from lean pork. Heavily seasoned and smoked, it provides a spicy smoked flavor to food cooked with it. Smoked ham may be substituted, but it will not provide the same smokiness or intensity. Tasso is available in Louisiana and some metropolitan areas; it can also be purchased from mail-order sources (see page 121).

     2 pounds small green beans,
        cut in 2-inch pieces
     1 cup unsalted butter
     1 cup tasso, chopped in
        ¼-inch dice
        Salt and pepper, to taste

Blanch beans in 1 gallon boiling, salted water for 3 minutes. Remove beans and plunge them into ice-cold water. Place butter in a medium skillet, then add tasso. Slowly fry tasso, being careful not to burn butter. Remove tasso and set aside. Sauté beans in butter remaining in skillet. After 1 to 2 minutes taste beans to see if they are tender. If so, remove beans from skillet; if not, continue to sauté a minute or two more. Salt and pepper to taste. To serve, combine green beans, butter, and tasso.

Serves 8 to 10.

PECAN PIE

This version of the southern favorite comes from the mid-South and is less sweet than many renditions prepared in the deep South. The recipe originally appeared in the California Culinary Academy series cookbook *Regional American Classics* and was contributed by Naomi Wise and Michael Goodwin.

     3 eggs, *lightly beaten*
     ¾ cup firmly packed
        dark brown sugar
     ½ cup white corn syrup
     1 tablespoon cider vinegar
     1 teaspoon vanilla extract
     2 tablespoons unsalted
        butter, melted
        Pinch salt
     1 cup pecans, coarsely chopped
     1 unbaked 9-inch pie shell,
        refrigerated
     1 cup (approximately) pecan
        halves
     1 cup whipping cream
        (optional)

1. Preheat oven to 425° F. In a medium bowl stir together eggs, sugar, corn syrup, vinegar, vanilla, butter, and salt. When mixture is well blended, stir in chopped pecans.

2. Pour mixture into pie shell. Arrange enough pecan halves side by side on surface of filling to cover in a sunburst design.

3. Place pie on lowest rack of oven. Immediately lower oven temperature to 350° F and bake until crust is lightly browned and filling sets (about 45 minutes). Place on a wire rack to cool before serving.

4. If whipped cream is desired for topping, beat cream with an electric beater until stiff peaks form when beater is lifted.

Serves 8.

Kids' Cooking

...THEIR DAY-AFTER-THANKSGIVING LUNCH

Using a water smoker is a bit tricky and best left to adults. But you can certainly help with food preparation, cleanup, and—of course—eating. The Thanksgiving menu (see page 70) was planned with plenty of leftovers in mind, and just about anyone can put together a sandwich. So, kids, give your folks a break after all their work smoking the turkey; make this easy meal yourself.

DAGWOOD SANDWICH

The biggest difficulty kids—or for that matter, adults—will have with this over-stuffed sandwich is getting their mouths open wide enough to bite into it. The term Dagwood comes from the *Blondie* comic strips, movies, and television shows. Mr. Dagwood Bumstead had a hard time eating the large sandwiches he would comically prepare. Once you taste these sandwiches you may look forward to Thanksgiving more for the leftovers than for the main meal!

> 2 slices sandwich bread,
> such as egg bread or crusty
> wheat bread
> Mayonnaise, to taste
> Leftover Italian Sausage
> and Fresh Fennel Stuffing
> (see page 73)
> Leftover Cranberry, Brandy,
> Apricot Sauce (see page 70)
> 2 to 4 slices Smoked Turkey
> With Soy-Ginger Marinade
> (see page 72)

Generously apply mayonnaise to both slices of bread. To one slice apply a layer of leftover stuffing. Over the stuffing spread some Cranberry, Brandy, Apricot Sauce, then a layer of turkey slices. Close sandwich and cut in half on the diagonal. Try eating from the corners inward; it makes things a little easier.

Makes 1 sandwich.

SOUR CREAM–SUGAR COOKIES

These crisp and tender cookies are the sort that everybody associates with the word *homemade*. This recipe, created by Cynthia Scheer, originally appeared in the California Culinary Academy series cookbook *Regional American Classics*. Note that the dough needs to chill at least 2 hours.

> ½ cup butter or margarine,
> softened
> 1¼ cups sugar
> 1 egg
> 1 teaspoon vanilla extract
> ½ teaspoon baking soda
> ½ cup sour cream
> 3 cups flour
> 1½ teaspoons baking powder
> ¼ teaspoon each *salt
> and ground nutmeg*
> *Chocolate sprinkles and
> additional sugar, for
> decoration*

1. In a large bowl beat butter until fluffy. Gradually add sugar, beating until light. Add egg and vanilla; beat again until fluffy. In a small bowl stir baking soda into sour cream. Blend into butter mixture.

2. In a medium bowl stir together 2 cups of the flour, the baking powder, salt, and nutmeg. Gradually blend flour mixture into butter mixture. Add the remaining flour, mixing in about ¼ cup at a time, until well combined.

3. Divide dough into 2 equal portions; enclose in plastic wrap and refrigerate until firm (about 2 hours or until next day).

4. Preheat oven to 375° F. Lightly grease baking sheets. Roll cookie dough out on a lightly floured board or pastry cloth until about ⅛ inch thick. Cut in 3-inch rounds or your favorite fancy shapes.

5. Place cookies on baking sheets about ½ inch apart. Sprinkle lightly with chocolate or sugar.

6. Bake until golden brown (8 to 10 minutes). Transfer to wire racks to cool before eating.

Makes about 4 dozen 3½-inch cookies.

A rectangular gas grill is so easy to use that you may find yourself barbecuing the year around. Use tanks or run an extra gas line from the house to fuel the grill.

Barbecuing

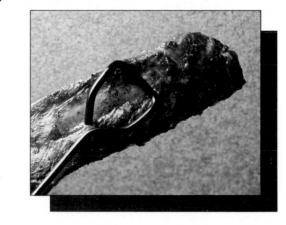

Ages ago someone decided to try slowly roasting freshly killed game over the fire, and so laid a foundation for centuries of delicious meals. Early explorers discovered that Native North Americans built a framework of green saplings over a slowly smoldering fire. On the frame they dried meat and fish. Spaniards called this "grill" *barbacoa,* a term used in Spanish to this day. French settlers slowly roasted whole animals from head to tail, that is, in French, *barbe-a-queue.* Whatever the origin, barbecue is an American institution with strong roots in many regions. This chapter explores many different barbecue styles, and features both traditional recipes and barbecue dishes with a modern twist.

BARBECUE DEFINED

Barbecue, barbeque, BBQ, Bar-b-que: There are many ways to spell the word and many regional variations on the cooking theme. People are fiercely proud of their own regional version as being "the best around." Indeed, some famous barbecue towns, such as Kansas City and Memphis, still have impassioned debates over the barbecue house that serves the most authentic barbecue. As varied as the different styles are, they all share several common traits. Barbecue is the art of slowly cooking large pieces of meat over a smoky, cool (about 225° F) fire. Most barbecue is served with a tangy sauce at the table to moisten and flavor the meat. Each area is home to a specific version, and versions vary from the simple sauce of North Carolina (which is made of cider vinegar and crushed red chiles) to the spicy vegetable-laden tomato sauces of the Southwest.

Barbecuing is different from grilling and smoking in that it imparts a distinctive smoke flavor and is served with a vinegar-based tangy sauce. Grilled and smoked foods possess a smoky flavor, but are served plain or with any one of a multitude of sauces. In general, grilled food is cooked more quickly than barbecued food, and the style and taste of grilled food is more varied. Smoked food tends to be more subtle in flavor than barbecued items, and smoked food is never served with a vinegar-based sauce. Of course most people aren't concerned about what barbecue is, just when they can get some more.

Pit-Smoked Barbecue

Most people agree that "authentic" barbecued food is pit-smoked. The term originated in the South, where long, hot summers forced people to roast meats outside. Meats were roasted in large pits in the ground, which were lined with stones or bricks. Large hardwood logs were laid in the pits and set on fire. When the wood burned down to a bed of coals, large pieces of meat (usually whole pigs) were lowered over the coals on a spit. The success of

the barbecue depended on the skill of the handlers (called pit masters) at maintaining an even, cool (about 225° F), and smoky fire. As the meat cooked, juices dripped on the fire and created a distinct smoked flavor in the meat. The meat and fire were carefully tended for 8 to 12 hours (sometimes for days), until the meat began to fall off the bone. The smoke-infused meat was removed and served in pieces or pulled from the bone with a fork. The crowning touch was the secret tangy sauce served at the table to moisten and flavor the meat.

There are few authentic outdoor pit houses around anymore, but the quality of the barbecue hasn't suffered. The pit is now a brick- or metal-lined oven that utilizes a slow-cooking method identical to the traditional process except that cooking is indoors. Many restaurants have switched to gas burners to economize on fuel and labor. Instead of large hardwood logs, presoaked hardwood chunks provide the essential smoke flavor in gas ovens. It is hard to duplicate the intense smoky flavor of a pit barbecue in your own backyard, but with a little practice, technique, and attention to detail, you can produce a wonderful barbecue at home.

BARBECUE EQUIPMENT AND TECHNIQUE

The type of equipment that you will need depends upon the size of meat to be barbecued. Barbecue recipes in this chapter were developed and tested on a covered gas grill. In most cases, a covered kettle-shaped grill also works beautifully. Cook spareribs, country ribs, beef ribs, beef short ribs, chicken, fish, ham, sausage, and any other small cuts by using the indirect-heat method of cooking as described on page 12. If you are cooking larger pieces of meat that require more than two hours to cook, a water smoker will work the best (see page 48). Briskets, pork shoulders, fresh hams, and pork butts all require longer, slower cooking.

The other equipment needed for barbecuing is about the same as that needed for grilling (see page 7). You may notice in the recipes the instruction to use non-aluminum pans. Most barbecue sauces contain acidic ingredients such as tomatoes, lemon juice, and vinegar. These acids produce a chemical reaction with aluminum that leaves a rather unpleasant flavor.

Converting a Gas Grill to a Water Smoker

Convert a gas grill into a water smoker by placing a pan of water over the center burner. Turn off the center burner, and turn the two outside burners to low. Place a pan of presoaked wood chips over one of the outside burners, and place the meat directly over the water pan. Close the lid, and adjust the outside burner temperatures as necessary to maintain an even temperature of 225° F. This method works perfectly well except that you don't get quite the intense smoked flavor that you do with a true water smoker.

Converting a Kettle-Shaped Grill to a Water Smoker

If you are particularly expert and somewhat adventurous with charcoal fires in a covered kettle-shaped grill, you can also use it for long, slow cooking. Bank all coals to one side of the kettle. On the other side place a water pan on the lower grill opposite the coals. Put presoaked hardwood chunks on the coals, and place the meat directly over the water pan. Add coals as necessary to maintain an even temperature of 225° F. Start with about 30 to 40 briquettes, and add about 12 per hour to keep the fire going. Recipes in this section were not tested using this method because of the difficulty of maintaining an even temperature.

The essential ingredients of a good barbecue are plenty of smoke and lots of time. If you rush things, you will end up with tough and dry food. Allow time for slow cooking and you will be rewarded with a succulent, tender barbecue.

REGIONAL DIFFERENCES

Every area of the country claims to have the best barbecue. Even within areas, there are intense disagreements about what makes "the best." Most people wouldn't dare admit it, but there really aren't substantial differences between regions. There is a wide difference between great barbecue and mediocre barbecue, but that has everything to do with who is cooking—not where they are cooking. Essentially, barbecues vary in three specific features: the type of wood used for smoke, the kind of meat most favored, and—most significant—the type of sauce served at the table.

You can understand the regional nature of barbecue by realizing that it originated by utilizing local ingredients. Until recently there weren't nationally marketed wood chips or barbecue sauces. Hardwoods of a particular region were used and imbued the meat with a distinctive flavor. In the East and Southeast oak and hickory were the standard; in the Northeast applewood, maple, and corncobs provided the flavor. In the deep South and the Midwest, pecan, oak, and hickory predominated. Texans used indigenous mesquite, oak, and pecan. Those in the Northwest used alderwood and California used the fruitwoods, oak, and manzanita that were readily available.

Pork is overwhelmingly the favorite barbecued food of Southerners. To them, whole pigs, pork shoulders, and spareribs are the only options. Floridians provide the exception to this southern preference; they add seafood to a barbecue feed. Southwestern barbecue traditions began with the cowboys, who cooked up a steer on their trail rides. To this day Texans swear by barbecued brisket. Beef ribs and spareribs are good, but the brisket is heavenly. The West Coast has become the melting pot of barbecue, with no one cut of meat dominating the cuisine.

Sauces are equally distinctive. North Carolina is split down the middle—each half has a favorite

sauce. Eastern North Carolina touts a deliciously simple sauce of cider vinegar and crushed red peppers poured over pulled barbecued pork. The western half joins with South Carolina in favoring a mustard-spiced, tangy tomato-based sauce. Florida has a sauce that reflects the fruit groves in the state: a delightfully tart tomato sauce made with limes and horseradish. The deep South used the regional abundance of sugar cane and molasses to create a thick, and sweet, tomato-based sauce. The Creole influence in Louisiana produced a much spicier version of the southern sauce. In the Southwest a great variety of chiles contributed to a hot sauce with complex flavors. Kansas City ended up somewhere between the deep South and Texas, with a thick, sweet, molasses-based tomato sauce made fiery hot with chiles. The West Coast benefited from a strong Asian influence and now boasts sauces made not from tomatoes but from fruits and vinegar. Hoisin, soy sauce, ginger, and garlic are common ingredients of a West Coast barbecue sauce.

Cooks from Texas, Kansas, and Tennessee each may claim to have the greatest barbecue, but perhaps they are unfamiliar with the barbecued wonders derived from Southeast Asia. Thailand, Malaysia, and Vietnam, too, have regional barbecuing specialties. Fish Sauce is a cornerstone of Thai cooking. Made from fermented anchovies, small fish, and salt, this sauce both tenderizes and flavors food. It is an important ingredient in marinating Thai Barbecue Spareribs (see page 86), shown here with Dipping Sauce.

... OF BARBECUE SAUCES

Sauces reflect both regional variety and individual taste. Families and barbecue houses jealously guard their "secret" recipe. Experiment with the recipes that follow and alter them to suit your own taste. Most of these recipes aren't spicy hot—this lets you taste the basic sauce for the balance of sweet and sour. Once satisfied with the base, you can spice it up with cayenne pepper, chiles, jalapeños, hot pepper sauce, or the like. If you are serving a lot of people, make a mild or moderately spicy sauce, then let the daring ones in the crowd spice up their plate by sprinkling on crushed cayenne pepper or hot pepper sauce. Barbecue sauces will keep in a covered jar for up to a week refrigerated and freeze well for several months.

GEORGIA SAUCE

Plain and easy to prepare, this sauce is a good choice for a mixed crowd with various tastes. For those who like hot food, put crushed red pepper and a bottle of hot sauce on the table. This sauce works equally well with beef, pork, chicken, and fish.

- 1½ cups tomato purée
- 1 cup cider vinegar
- ½ cup oil
- ⅓ cup Worcestershire sauce
- ½ cup firmly packed dark brown sugar
- ¼ cup molasses
- 3 tablespoons mustard
- 2 teaspoons minced garlic
- 1 lemon, juiced

In a large non-aluminum saucepan, combine all ingredients. Slowly simmer for 15 minutes. Stir often to prevent sauce from burning. Allow sauce to rest for at least 1 hour after cooking to allow flavors to meld. Store in covered container in refrigerator until used.

Makes 3 cups.

NORTH CAROLINA SAUCE

In eastern North Carolina barbecue is taken very seriously. The simplicity of slowly roasted meat is accented only with the addition of crushed red peppers and cider vinegar—you won't find tomato sauce. At the table there is always a bottle of plain cider vinegar next to the bottle of barbecue sauce.

- 1 cup cider vinegar
- 2 tablespoons crushed red pepper
- 1 teaspoon liquid hot pepper sauce

Place all ingredients in a small plastic or glass container. Cover and shake well to combine. Store in refrigerator until used.

Makes 1 cup.

TEXAS SAUCE

This is a very rich and complexly flavored sauce full of vegetables and perfumed with chile powder and a hint of cumin. Oddly enough, there is no mustard in this sauce, so the flavor of tomato comes out more distinctly than in many barbecue sauces. This sauce is an excellent choice for beef, pork, and chicken. Don't use it on fish—it will easily overpower the delicate flavor.

- ½ cup butter
- 1 cup finely chopped onion
- 1 cup finely chopped celery
- 2 teaspoons minced garlic
- 1 cup tomato purée
- ½ cup cider vinegar
- ½ cup firmly packed dark brown sugar
- 1 cup beef stock
- ¼ cup Worcestershire sauce
- 2 bay leaves
- 2 teaspoons freshly ground black pepper
- 2 teaspoons cayenne pepper
- 1 teaspoon ground cumin
- 2 teaspoons chile powder
    Salt, to taste

In a large non-aluminum saucepan, melt butter and sauté onion, celery, and garlic until soft (about 10 minutes). Add remaining ingredients and slowly simmer for about 30 minutes. Stir frequently so that sauce doesn't burn. Allow sauce to rest for at least 1 hour so that flavors meld. Store covered in refrigerator. This sauce is even better the following day.

Makes 4 cups.

KANSAS CITY SAUCE

In Kansas City they love smoke and they love a thick and sweet sauce. The liquid smoke flavoring re-creates the smoky flavor of meat slowly smoked in the famous Kansas City barbecue pits. Catsup, molasses, and yellow mustard combine to lay the foundation for this thick all-American sauce. If you like spicy barbecue, try adding 1 to 2 tablespoons ground cayenne pepper. This sauce works well with beef, pork, or chicken; it would overpower fish.

- ½ cup oil
- 1 onion, finely chopped
- ½ green bell pepper, finely chopped
- 2 teaspoons minced garlic
- 1 bottle (16 oz) catsup
- ½ cup molasses
- 2 teaspoons hot pepper sauce
- ¼ cup yellow mustard
- 2 tablespoons cider vinegar
- ½ cup firmly packed dark brown sugar
- 4 tablespoons Worcestershire sauce
- 1 teaspoon liquid smoke flavor
- ¼ cup fresh lemon juice

Place oil in a large non-aluminum saucepan, then sauté onion, green pepper, and garlic until soft (about 10 minutes). Add remaining ingredients and continue to simmer slowly for 20 to 30 minutes. Stir frequently to prevent sauce from burning. Let rest for at least 1 hour after cooking to allow the flavors to meld.

Makes 4 cups.

LOUISIANA SAUCE

In Louisiana barbecue sauce begins in the same manner as other Creole sauces by employing the classic combination of onions, celery, green bell peppers, tomato, and garlic. The Creole recipe adds thyme and oregano at this point; create a barbecue sauce by adding molasses, brown sugar, and vinegar. This recipe produces a spicy, thick, complexly flavored sauce suitable for almost any cut of beef, pork, chicken, or fish. Louisiana natives may add more cayenne than this recipe calls for to make a memorably fiery sauce.

1   cup oil
2   cups finely chopped onion
1   large green bell pepper, finely chopped
1   cup finely chopped celery
2   tablespoons minced garlic
16 ounces tomato purée
1   tablespoon Creole or Dijon mustard
¼   cup white vinegar
4   teaspoons cayenne pepper
1   teaspoon hot pepper sauce
1   bay leaf
2   teaspoons freshly ground black pepper
½   cup firmly packed dark brown sugar
¼   cup dark molasses

Place oil in a large non-aluminum saucepan, then sauté onion, bell pepper, celery, and garlic until soft (about 10 minutes). Add remainder of ingredients and simmer slowly for 10 to 15 minutes, stirring frequently to avoid burning. Adjust seasoning to taste by altering amounts of sugar, spices, and vinegar. Cook an additional 5 to 10 minutes after changing seasoning. Let rest for at least 1 hour after cooking to allow flavors to meld. Store covered in refrigerator. Sauce is even better the next day.

Makes 6 cups.

BOURBON SAUCE

This sauce works equally well as a basting sauce and as a marinade. The alcohol evaporates as the sauce cooks, leaving a mysterious and intense bittersweet flavor. To use as a marinade, coat meat and leave covered in the refrigerator for 8 to 12 hours. Continue to baste with sauce as meat cooks, but don't serve this on the side—it is really only suitable if cooked into the meat. Sauce works best with pork and beef.

2   tablespoons lard
1   onion, finely chopped
1   tablespoon minced garlic
14 ounces tomato purée
½   cup Worcestershire sauce
2   tablespoons cider vinegar
½   cup yellow mustard
½   cup firmly packed brown sugar
¼   cup bourbon
2   tablespoons each *hot red chile powder and mild red chile powder*
2   drops liquid smoke flavor

Place lard in a large non-aluminum saucepan and sauté onion and garlic until soft (about 10 minutes). Add remaining ingredients and continue to cook for an additional 30 minutes. If you can't find the two strengths of chile powder, substitute 3 tablespoons ground cayenne pepper total. Stir frequently to prevent sauce from burning. Allow to rest for at least 1 hour before using.

Makes 3 cups.

KING SAUCE

This recipe was contributed by Oakland, California, artist John King. The nature of the sauce is predominately Asian, but there are a few interesting western touches. Use this sauce as a marinade for your barbecue and as a basting sauce. Rub the sauce into the meat and refrigerate covered for 8 to 12 hours. This sauce goes particularly well with pork and beef but can also be used with chicken and fish.

1   bottle (16 oz) hoisin sauce
1   cup soy sauce
2   tablespoons each *white vinegar and dry sherry*
4   tablespoons sesame oil
4   tablespoons Dijon mustard
3   tablespoons minced garlic
1   lemon, juiced
    Pepper, to taste
1   teaspoon ground cumin
2   teaspoons fennel seed, crushed
2   tablespoons mirin
⅓   cup orange juice

In a large bowl combine all ingredients and mix well. Adjust sauce to taste by altering individual amounts of each ingredient. The flavors tend to dilute considerably during cooking, so keep them strong.

Makes 8 cups.

FLORIDA SAUCE

This unusual barbecue sauce includes horseradish and lime juice. It is tangy and sweet, with a delicate taste and a short shelf life. Try to make this the same day as your barbecue because the flavors tend to fade quickly. This sauce is excellent on fish and chicken, and interesting on pork. It is too delicate to match with beef ribs.

1   cup unsalted butter
½   cup firmly packed dark brown sugar
1   cup tomato purée
½   cup cider vinegar
6   ounces prepared horseradish
½   cup fresh lime juice
1   tablespoon Worcestershire sauce
2   teaspoons hot pepper sauce

In a large non-aluminum saucepan, melt butter and add remaining ingredients. Simmer slowly for 20 to 25 minutes, stirring frequently to prevent sauce from burning. Sauce can be used immediately.

Makes 4 cups.

BEEF BARBECUE

When people talk about beef and barbecue, they are talking about either ribs or brisket. There are basically two kinds of beef ribs suitable for barbecuing. The first come off the prime rib and are commonly known just as beef ribs. The second come off the chuck and are known as short ribs. Beef ribs are quite tender and can be cooked with or without a marinade over direct heat. Short ribs should always be cooked over indirect heat, and they benefit greatly from a marinade. By far the best choice for beef barbecue is beef ribs. They offer more meat, less fat, and can be cooked quickly until they are charred on the outside and juicy-rare on the inside. Short ribs should be cooked slowly until they begin to fall apart; faster cooking results in a tough and overly chewy rib.

When Texans talk about barbecue, they're talking brisket. The brisket is cooked slowly, heavily smoked with mesquite, and so tender you can cut it with a fork. The brisket is never basted. Sauce is usually served on the side at the table, although purists insist that sauce on a well-smoked brisket is a sacrilege. Of course, cooks in many areas of the country barbecue the brisket (particularly in Kansas City); they just don't crow about it as much as Texans do.

ROBERT'S BEEF BRISKET

This recipe comes from my father, who spent many a Sunday in Texas slowly tending his brisket over a mesquite fire. We always ate it plain, without any sauce. The brisket was mouthwateringly tender and laden with a delicious mesquite flavor. If you would rather serve it with a barbecue sauce, Texas Sauce (see page 80) is an excellent accompaniment. A water smoker is recommended to maintain a slow cooking temperature and to achieve the maximum smoked flavor. If you don't have a water smoker, use a gas grill set up as a water smoker as described on page 78. A kettle-shaped grill is not recommended for this recipe because it is difficult to maintain a low cooking temperature for such a long time.

1 beef brisket (20 to 25 lb), untrimmed, deckle on

1. Have a butcher cut a fresh brisket off the forequarter, leaving on the deckle (the rib bones) and all the fat cover. This is very important because the bones and fat keep the brisket moist during cooking.

2. Prepare fire for indirect-heat method of cooking. If using a water smoker, see page 46 for instructions. If using a gas grill, set it up as described on page 78. Use either mesquite charcoal or mesquite chips for flavor.

3. When fire is ready and brisket is at room temperature, place brisket on grill with bones on the bottom. You won't need to touch brisket for the duration of the cooking period. For the next 12 hours, make sure the fire maintains an even temperature of 225° F and that the mesquite chips are replenished.

4. Brisket is done when it begins to slide off bones and meat easily comes apart with a fork. Remove brisket from fire, being careful to leave it intact. Cover with aluminum foil and let rest for 30 minutes. To carve, remove bones from the bottom and fat cover from the top. There should be 8 to 10 pounds of pure meat. Slice against the grain and serve immediately.

Serves 15 to 20.

SESAME BEEF RIBS

Start this dish the day before serving it by marinating the ribs overnight. Most of the flavoring is accomplished in the marinating, which tenderizes the meat and imbues it with hints of sesame and the sweet fragrance of garlic. Use a mesquite fire to round out the flavors. Meat is cooked in just 15 minutes and is crispy outside and rare and tender at the bone.

> *2 green onions, finely chopped*
> *1 teaspoon minced garlic*
> *¼ cup soy sauce*
> *¼ cup sesame oil*
> *¼ cup rice wine vinegar*
> *2 teaspoons sesame seed*
> *2 tablespoons sugar*
> *1 teaspoon dry mustard*
> *1 teaspoon freshly ground pepper*
> *4 pounds trimmed beef ribs*

1. Prepare marinade by combining green onions, garlic, soy sauce, sesame oil, vinegar, sesame seed, sugar, mustard, and pepper. Score ribs almost to the bone every ½ inch. Rub in marinade, cover, and refrigerate 8 to 12 hours. Turn ribs several times to marinate evenly.

2. Prepare fire for direct-heat method of cooking (see page 12). Remove ribs from marinade and reserve marinade. Allow ribs to come to room temperature. Place ribs on grill over hot fire and close lid. Turn ribs several times during cooking and baste with reserved marinade. Ribs are done when they have a crispy exterior (about 15 minutes). Serve immediately.

Serves 4.

Sesame Beef Ribs are a good
weeknight dinner since most
of the work is done ahead.
Pair with make-ahead Golden
Potato Salad (see page 88).

This slab of Slow-Cooked Spareribs (opposite page) shown with Kansas City Sauce can easily feed two or three hungry people. Allow plenty of time to cook the ribs: The slower you go, the better they taste. For greater variety, substitute other tomato-based Barbecue Sauces (see page 80) and try different combinations of wood chips for the coals.

THAI SHORT RIBS

This recipe uses the same marinade used for Thai Barbecued Spareribs with Dipping Sauce (see page 86). Any sauce that does not have a tomato base can be substituted, such as King Sauce (see page 81) or North Carolina Sauce (see page 80). Serve with sesame noodles and a cold, sweet carrot salad for an authentic Southeast Asian meal.

> 1 cup marinade from Thai
>   Barbecued Spareribs
>   (see page 86)
> 4 pounds short ribs
> 1 cup Dipping Sauce
>   (see page 86)

1. In a large mixing bowl, massage marinade into ribs. Cover and refrigerate for 8 to 12 hours.

2. Prepare fire for indirect-heat method of cooking (see page 12). If using a gas grill, presoak hardwood chips. If using a charcoal grill, presoak hardwood chunks. When fire is ready, place hardwood chips or chunks onto fire. Allow fire to cool to an even cooking temperature of 225° F.

3. Remove ribs from marinade and reserve marinade. Wipe excess marinade from ribs. Brown ribs over direct heat on both sides (about 5 minutes per side). Place ribs over indirect heat. Baste with reserved marinade and turn ribs over about every 15 minutes. Ribs are done when they begin to fall off bone (1 to 1½ hours of cooking). Serve with Dipping Sauce.

Serves 4.

TEXAS BEEF RIBS

Although brisket is the overwhelming favorite of most Texans when it comes to barbecue, there is a sizable following for beef ribs. You might want to add 2 more teaspoons cayenne to really jazz up the barbecue sauce.

> 4 pounds trimmed beef ribs
> 1 cup Texas Sauce (see page 80)

1. Prepare fire for direct-heat method of cooking (see page 12). If using a gas grill, presoak hardwood chips. If using a charcoal grill, presoak hardwood chunks. When fire is ready, place hardwood chips or wood chunks onto fire.

2. Place ribs on grill over hot fire and brown ribs on both sides, 3 to 4 minutes per side. When ribs are browned, baste with Texas Sauce and cover. After 3 minutes baste and turn ribs again. Be careful of flare-ups—tomato sauce and rib drippings will incite the fire. Control flare-ups with the spray of a water bottle and by closing the lid of the grill. Ribs are done when nearly black on the outside, about 15 minutes. Serve immediately.

Serves 4.

PORK BARBECUE

Pork is probably the ideal meat for barbecue. There is enough internal fat to keep the meat moist and flavorful during cooking. Pork accepts sauces and marinades well, particularly the sweet and tangy flavors central to a good barbecue sauce. Any cut of pork is suitable for barbecue; indeed, the best "cut" of all is the whole pig. Spareribs, baby back ribs, country ribs, pork shoulder, and pork butt are all excellent barbecued.

When it comes to spareribs, many questions arise concerning the best way to create a tender, succulent offering. There really isn't any great mystery about producing a fabulous rib every time. The most important thing to remember is to always cook ribs over low, indirect heat. This allows a relatively tough piece of meat to become tender while remaining juicy. Don't boil the ribs beforehand; just cook them slowly until you can easily pull the ribs apart with your hands. The second trick is to wait until the ribs are halfway done before basting with a tomato-based barbecue sauce. If you baste them earlier, the sauce burns before the ribs are done. Don't worry, there is plenty of time for the sauce to penetrate the meat. The recipes for spareribs that follow work equally well with baby back ribs.

If you really want to splurge, try cooking up a savory marinated country rib. Country ribs are the rib end of a pork loin butterflied open and are a bit more expensive than spareribs. However, you end up with a very tender piece of pork that usually weighs 5 to 6 pounds—and nearly all of it is meat. Country ribs should be slowly cooked over indirect heat, and can be basted with a tomato-based sauce or marinated beforehand. The marinade is used only to flavor the meat—the ribs are tender already.

Large pieces of pork, such as the shoulder, butt, or whole pig, require up to 8 hours of cooking time. A Pit-Roasted Pork Shoulder is featured in the North Carolina Barbecue menu, which begins on page 93.

HOISIN SPARERIBS

Marinating imbues tremendous flavor to the ribs as well as tenderizing them. Do not use a tomato-based sauce, which would burn. In this recipe the aromatic touch of five-spice powder combines with the full-bodied sweetness of hoisin sauce to create a luscious flavor. It is best to marinate the ribs for 8 to 12 hours in your refrigerator, but you can get away with 2 hours at room temperature. Hoisin sauce is sold canned in the foreign-food section of most supermarkets. This recipe works equally well with other marinades, such as King Sauce (see page 80).

> 1 slab pork spareribs
> (about 3½ lb)
> ¼ cup hoisin sauce
> ¼ cup sugar
> ¼ cup Shaoxing or dry sherry
> 1 teaspoon Chinese
> five-spice powder
> ¼ cup sesame oil

1. Have the butcher crack the "wing" of the spareribs so that after cooking you can cut between bones easily. In a shallow baking pan big enough for the spareribs to lie flat in, combine hoisin sauce, sugar, Shaoxing, five-spice powder, and sesame oil. Cover ribs on both sides with marinade. Cover pan and refrigerate for 8 to 12 hours.

2. Prepare fire for indirect-heat method of cooking (see page 12). Allow fire to cool until achieving a cooking temperature of about 225° F. Remove meat from marinade, blot off excess marinade, and place ribs on grill over drip pan. Close lid and cook until ribs pull apart easily with your fingers (about 45 minutes). Be sure to turn ribs over several times during cooking. Remove ribs from grill and let rest for 5 minutes to retain juices, then slice between the bones to serve.

Serves 2 or 3.

SLOW-COOKED SPARERIBS

When choosing spareribs, always insist on very fresh pork. The meat should be bright, dry, and free of any odor. Have the butcher crack the "wing bone" with a cleaver so that you can easily cut between the ribs. Always cook ribs whole to maintain juiciness. Try experimenting with different flavored wood chips or chunks. With ribs the more smoked flavor, the better. This recipe works well with any tomato-based barbecue sauce. Particularly good choices are Louisiana Sauce, Texas Sauce, Kansas City Sauce, and Georgia Sauce.

> 1 slab pork spareribs (3 to 4 lb)
> 2 cups barbecue sauce
> (see page 80)

1. Prepare fire for indirect-heat method of cooking. Allow coals to cool down to a moderate temperature. Add presoaked wood chips or chunks to coals. When fire is ready, place ribs directly over coals to lightly brown on both sides (3 to 4 minutes per side). Move ribs over drip pan and close lid. Close vents as necessary to achieve a constant temperature of 225° F. If fire is still too hot, remove ribs until temperature drops.

2. Place half the barbecue sauce in a saucepan and heat for later use as a condiment; use the other half for basting. When ribs are halfway done (in about 30 minutes) lay a piece of heavy-duty aluminum foil under them. Use a fork to pierce foil 10 times, distributing the pokes evenly so that smoke continues to penetrate ribs. Baste with barbecue sauce on top side. Close lid. In 5 minutes baste top again and flip ribs over; now baste the other side. Continue this process of basting and flipping until ribs pull apart easily with your fingers (after about 1 hour total of cooking time).

3. Remove ribs from fire and cut between bones with a knife. Serve immediately with reserved hot barbecue sauce.

Serves 2 or 3.

THAI BARBECUED SPARERIBS WITH DIPPING SAUCE

This recipe was contributed by San Francisco Barbecue, a popular Thai restaurant specializing in barbecue where patrons can order barbecued chicken, spareribs, beef ribs, or oysters. Although many Thai restaurants are noted for fiery hot cuisine, this one is known for subtly flavored and perfectly done ribs. Fish sauce is available in the foreign-food section of most supermarkets.

½ cup fish sauce
¼ cup sugar
2 teaspoons salt
1 tablespoon pepper
2 tablespoons minced garlic
1 tablespoon chopped cilantro
½ cup water
2 slabs (6 to 7 lb total) pork spareribs

Dipping Sauce

⅔ cup sugar
½ cup distilled vinegar
2 teaspoons salt
2 tablespoons minced garlic
1 red bell pepper

1. In a large mixing bowl, combine fish sauce, sugar, salt, pepper, garlic, cilantro, and the water. Place ribs in bowl and massage marinade into meat with your hands. Cover and refrigerate for 8 to 12 hours.

2. Prepare fire for direct-heat method of cooking (see page 12). These ribs can be cooked over direct heat because marinade tenderizes meat. If using a gas grill, presoak hardwood chips. If using a charcoal grill, presoak hardwood chunks. When fire is ready, place chips or chunks on fire. Remove meat from marinade, wipe off excess marinade, and reserve marinade in bowl. Place ribs on grill and brown on both sides (about 5 minutes per side). Baste ribs and close lid. Baste and turn over ribs every 10 minutes until done, about 45 minutes total cooking time. Slice between bones and serve immediately with Dipping Sauce.

Serves 6 to 8.

Dipping Sauce In a small saucepan combine sugar, vinegar, salt, and garlic. Bring to a boil, and reduce heat to a simmer. Cook until thick (about 5 minutes). Finely grate red pepper and add to sauce for color right before serving.

Makes 1 cup.

KING COUNTRY RIBS

This recipe utilizes Oakland, California, artist John King's hoisin-based sauce. Any other barbecue sauce without a tomato base can be substituted (see page 80), as well as the Dipping Sauce from Thai Barbecued Spareribs (see at left). It is best to marinate the ribs for 8 to 12 hours in the refrigerator so that the flavors can fully penetrate the meat.

1 piece country ribs (5 to 6 lb)
2 cups King Sauce (see page 81)

1. Place ribs in non-aluminum bowl or baking pan. Massage King Sauce into meat with your hands. Cover and refrigerate for 8 to 12 hours.

2. Prepare fire for indirect-heat method of cooking (see page 12). If using a gas grill, presoak hardwood chips. If using a charcoal grill, presoak hardwood chunks. When fire is ready, put chips or chunks onto fire. Allow cooking temperature to cool to an even 225° F. Remove ribs from bowl and rub off excess sauce. Reserve sauce. Brown ribs over direct heat on both sides (about 5 minutes per side). Place ribs over indirect heat, bone side down. Baste ribs with reserved sauce and close lid. Be careful to maintain a constant cooking temperature of 225° F. Baste ribs about every 10 minutes. After 30 minutes flip ribs over. Continue to cook another 30 minutes, basting and flipping ribs every 10 minutes. Ribs should be done in 1 to 1½ hours of total cooking time. Remove meat from fire and let rest for 10 minutes to retain juices. Slice between bones and serve immediately. Serving sauce at the table is considered optional—it is very strong and works best as a marinade.

Serves 6 to 8.

TEXAS COUNTRY RIBS

Country ribs marry well with a hearty tomato-based barbecue sauce. This recipe utilizes Texas Sauce, although Louisiana Sauce, Kansas City Sauce, Georgia Sauce, Florida Sauce, or your favorite tomato-based sauce would all be equally suitable. Have the kids whip up one of the summer salads (see page 88) for a family dinner.

1 piece country ribs (5 to 6 lb)
2 cups Texas Sauce

1. Prepare fire for indirect-heat method of cooking (see page 12). If using a gas grill, presoak hardwood chips. If using a charcoal grill, presoak hardwood chunks. When fire is ready, place hardwood chips or chunks on fire. Allow fire to cool to an even 225° F. Sear ribs on both sides over direct heat, about 5 minutes per side. Then place meat over indirect heat, bone side down, and close lid. Watch cooking temperature carefully, and make any adjustments necessary to maintain 225° F. Use one-half of Texas Sauce for basting and reserve remainder to serve hot as a condiment.

2. After 30 minutes place a piece of heavy-duty aluminum foil under ribs. Pierce foil about 12 times with a fork, distributing pokes evenly to allow smoke to penetrate meat. Lavishly baste meat side of ribs with Texas Sauce. Close lid and continue to monitor cooking temperature and smoke supply (the more the better). After 10 minutes turn ribs over and baste rib side. Continue turning and basting every 10 minutes until ribs are done (1 to 1½ hours of total cooking). Remove from fire and let rest for 10 minutes so that ribs retain juices. Slice between bones and serve with warmed Texas Sauce.

Serves 6 to 8.

East meets West in a pork dish basted with hoisin-flavored sauce. Start King Country Ribs one day before serving to allow for the longer-than-average marination.

2. Have your parents help you whip the cream in a medium-sized bowl using a whisk or an electric mixer. After 5 minutes, if using an electric mixer, add sugar. Mix until peaks form (about 10 minutes if using an electric mixer).

3. Using a rubber spatula scrape whipped cream onto top of fruit mixture. Carefully mix fruit and whipped cream together. Serve right away or cover and keep in the refrigerator until it's time to eat.

Serves 6.

DIANNE'S FRUIT SALAD

Along with not having to go to school, eating fresh fruit is one of the major joys of summer. Fruit served with yogurt and then rolled in brown sugar makes this special treat even better. Use your favorite fruits or the ones listed here.

- 2 peaches, washed, pitted, and cut into wedges
  Juice of ½ lemon
- 1 cup plain yogurt
- ½ cup firmly packed dark brown sugar
- 3 plums, washed, pitted, and cut into quarters
- 1 pint strawberries (1 basket), washed
- 1 bunch seedless grapes, washed
- 6 wedges watermelon, about 1½ inch thick
- 2 navel oranges, peeled and sectioned

1. In a bowl pour lemon juice over cut peaches so that they don't turn brown.

2. Put yogurt and brown sugar into individual dipping bowls. Place in center of a serving platter; decoratively arrange fruit around bowls. Keep chilled in refrigerator until serving time.

3. To eat, pick up pieces of fruit with fingers or tooth picks. Dip first into yogurt, then into brown sugar, then pop into your mouth.

Serves 6.

Kids' Cooking

. . . SUMMER SALADS

This section is for all the kids who want to help out during a backyard barbecue. Slowly cooked barbecue is a fairly advanced cooking technique that is tricky for even many adults. You can best help by preparing the side dishes that go along with the barbecued food. The following classic salads require only basic cooking skills. The recipes can be made the day before or the morning of the barbecue. Make sure an adult approves your working in the kitchen and, at least the first time, make sure one is around in case you need help. But, try to figure out how to make these salads yourself. You will be proud of the delicious results.

ELAINE'S AMBROSIA SALAD

This classic southern-style sweet fruit salad is shown in the above photograph. It has been enjoyed by both kids and adults over the years. Although it is called a salad, you may want to have it for dessert. It should be made the day you plan to eat it, since whipped cream tends to get watery the next day. For a nice variation, try adding 1 cup of halved seedless grapes or 1 cup of stemmed, quartered fresh strawberries.

- 3 navel oranges, peeled and cut into bite-sized pieces
- 1½ cups canned pineapple chunks, drained
- 2 bananas, cut into bite-sized pieces
- ½ cup miniature marshmallows
- ½ cup drained, chopped maraschino cherries
- ½ cup flaked coconut
- 1 cup whipping cream
- 2 tablespoons confectioners' sugar

1. In a large bowl lightly mix, using your hands, oranges, pineapples, bananas, marshmallows, cherries, and coconut until well blended. Be careful not to squash the bananas.

JOSIE'S FRUIT DELIGHT

You can prepare this dish without any parental help, and probably won't need their help to eat it either. After you have made this dish a few times, try making it in a fun-shaped mold. Getting the gelatin out of the mold is a little tricky at first, but once you have mastered it, everyone will be quite impressed with your results.

- 1 box (3 oz) strawberry-flavored gelatin mix
- 1 box (3 oz) lime-flavored gelatin mix
- 2 cups boiling water
- 1 can (8 oz) fruit cocktail and juices
- 1 cup sour cream
- ½ cup mashed bananas

1. In a mixing bowl combine strawberry-flavored gelatin mix and 1 cup of the boiling water until gelatin is dissolved. Stir in fruit cocktail with juices. Pour into an 8-inch pan and place in refrigerator to chill.

2. In a mixing bowl combine lime-flavored gelatin mix and 1 cup of the boiling water until gelatin is dissolved. Place in refrigerator to chill.

3. In a mixing bowl stir sour cream and bananas with a whisk until smooth. Set aside.

4. When both gelatins are partially set (after about 1 hour in the refrigerator), spread sour cream mixture on top of strawberry gelatin. Pour lime gelatin mixture on top of sour cream. Place pan in refrigerator until gelatin is fully congealed (about 3 hours). Serve chilled.

Serves 6.

Note To get gelatin out of a mold, fill a pan larger than your mold pan with very hot water. Wear oven mitts on both hands and, holding the top edges of the mold, quickly dip the bottom of the mold pan into and out of the pan of hot water. Set the mold pan on the counter. Put a plate on top of the mold pan and flip the mold and the plate over. The gelatin should slip right out of the mold pan and right onto the plate.

SWEET-SOUR MACARONI SALAD

This creamy salad is easy and quick. It takes less than an hour to make and needs only an hour for the flavors to blend. Macaroni is great with pork dishes. Use a chutney such as Major Grey's brand. This classic pasta salad and the potato salad following it were developed by Cynthia Scheer for the California Culinary Academy series book *Salads*.

- 1 package (8 oz) salad macaroni
- ½ cup mayonnaise
- ¼ cup sour cream
- 1 tablespoon each *sugar and cider vinegar*
- ¼ cup chutney, chopped
- 1 stalk celery, finely chopped
- ½ cup diced baked ham
- 1 jar (2 oz) diced pimientos, drained
  Chopped parsley, for garnish

1. Cook macaroni according to directions on package. Drain into a colander set in the sink. Rinse with cold water and drain again. Set aside.

2. Prepare dressing in a large bowl by mixing mayonnaise, sour cream, sugar, vinegar, and chutney until smooth.

3. Add macaroni, celery, ham, and pimientos. Turn lightly to coat all ingredients with dressing. Cover and refrigerate for at least 1 hour to blend flavors.

4. Sprinkle parsley on top before serving.

Serves 4 to 6.

GOLDEN POTATO SALAD

Make this the day before you want to eat it because it takes some time for the flavors to blend.

- 4 large smooth-skinned potatoes (2 to 2½ lb)
- ½ teaspoon salt
- 3 tablespoons sherry vinegar
  Dash ground white pepper
- 1 small clove garlic, minced or pressed
- ¼ cup oil
- ⅓ cup each *mayonnaise and sour cream*
- 1½ tablespoons mustard
- 1 teaspoon horseradish
- ¼ teaspoon celery seed
- ¼ cup each *chopped sweet pickle and sliced green onion*
- 1 small green pepper, seeded and finely chopped
- 3 hard-cooked eggs, peeled and sliced

1. Scrub potatoes and place unpeeled in a large pot. Cover with water, add ½ teaspoon of the salt, and cook over high heat until they boil. Turn down heat and set lid slightly ajar (to let the steam escape); boil until potatoes are tender (35 to 40 minutes). Drain into a colander set in the sink. While potatoes are warm, slip off skins and cut potatoes into ¾-inch cubes. Place cubes in a large bowl.

2. In a small bowl mix vinegar, ½ teaspoon of the salt, pepper, garlic, and oil by using a whisk or fork. Gradually pour oil mixture over potatoes, turning potatoes gently until all are coated. Cover and refrigerate for 2 to 12 hours.

3. From 1 to 3 hours before serving, prepare the dressing in a small bowl by mixing mayonnaise, sour cream, mustard, horseradish, celery seed, and ¼ teaspoon of the salt. Take potatoes from refrigerator and pour dressing over them. Add pickle, onion, green pepper, and eggs slices. Gently mix all ingredients together. Put into a serving bowl. Cover and refrigerate for another 1 to 3 hours before serving.

Serves 6 to 8.

CHICKEN BARBECUE

Chicken is possibly the easiest and most versatile food to barbecue. Since chicken accepts most flavors as an artist's canvas accepts any colors, you can use just about any barbecue sauce that you desire. The secrets are to cook the chicken slowly with plenty of smoke, and don't baste the chicken with a tomato-based sauce until chicken is halfway done.

BOURBON CHICKEN

In this recipe the marinade is used as a barbecue sauce. Any sauce that has a tomato base can be substituted for the Bourbon Sauce.

> 1 chicken (3 to 4 lb), cut into individual pieces
> 2 cups Bourbon Sauce (see page 80)

1. Wash chicken and pat dry. In a large bowl massage Bourbon Sauce into chicken with your hands. Cover and refrigerate for 8 to 12 hours.

2. Prepare fire for indirect-heat method of cooking (see page 12). If using a gas grill, use presoaked hardwood chips. If using a charcoal fire, use presoaked hardwood chunks. When fire is ready, place hardwood chips or chunks onto fire. Allow fire to cool to an even cooking temperature of 225° F.

3. Remove chicken from sauce; reserve sauce. Remove excess sauce from chicken. Brown chicken on all sides over direct heat (about 5 minutes per side). Place chicken over indirect heat and close lid. After 10 minutes and every 10 minutes after that, baste chicken with reserved sauce and turn over. Total cooking time is 45 minutes to 1 hour. Serve immediately. Sauce is quite strong, so serving it on the side is optional.

Serves 3 or 4.

BUFFALO WINGS

This easy dish makes a wonderful appetizer when served to a crowd. The chicken wings can be marinated the day before, and grilled at the last minute. Try serving with Creole Skewers With Mustard Butter (see page 29) at your next big party. And to think you didn't even know buffaloes could fly!

> 1 cup apple cider vinegar
> Juice of 1 lemon
> 2 teaspoons cayenne pepper
> 1 teaspoon ground cumin
> 1 tablespoon Worcestershire sauce
> 1 teaspoon liquid hot pepper sauce
> 2 tablespoons sugar
> 1 teaspoon salt
> 1 teaspoon coarse, freshly ground pepper
> 4 pounds chicken wings
> Oil, for grill

Chili Dipping Sauce

> ⅔ cup plain yogurt
> ½ teaspoon ground cumin
> 1 teaspoon chili powder
> 1 teaspoon minced garlic
> Juice of 1 lemon
> 1 teaspoon Dijon mustard
> Salt and pepper, to taste

1. In a large mixing bowl, combine all ingredients except the chicken and the oil.

2. Wash chicken under cold water and pat dry. Place chicken in marinade, cover, and refrigerate for 8 to 12 hours.

3. Prepare fire for direct-heat method of cooking (see page 12). Remove chicken from marinade (reserving marinade) and wipe off excess marinade. When fire is hot, oil grill and place chicken on grill. Close lid and cook until crispy and golden brown (30 to 40 minutes). During cooking, turn frequently and baste with marinade. Serve with Chili Dipping Sauce.

Serves 6.

Chili Dipping Sauce Combine all ingredients. Adjust flavoring to taste.

Makes ¾ cup.

GEORGIA CHICKEN

Georgia Sauce gives chicken a sweet and mild flavor. Substitute any tomato-based sauce if you desire. Serve this dish on a hot summer evening with pasta salad (as seen at right) or Parker's Coleslaw (see page 94), corn on the cob, freshly squeezed lemonade, and a few of Georgia's own peaches.

> 1 chicken (3 to 4 lb), cut into individual pieces
> ¼ cup oil
> 2 cups Georgia Sauce (see page 80)

1. Prepare fire for indirect-heat method of cooking (see page 12). If using a gas grill, use presoaked hardwood chips. If using a charcoal grill, use presoaked hardwood chunks. Wash chicken and pat dry. Coat chicken with oil.

2. When fire is ready, put hardwood chips or chunks on fire. Allow to cool to a cooking temperature of 225° F. Lightly brown chicken on all sides over direct heat, about 5 minutes per side. Move chicken over indirect heat and close lid. Closely monitor fire to maintain proper cooking temperature. After 15 minutes, turn chicken over. Use ½ Georgia Sauce for basting and reserve remainder to serve hot as a condiment.

3. After another 15 minutes place a piece of heavy-duty aluminum foil under chicken. Prick foil with fork in about 12 places to allow smoke to penetrate meat. Baste chicken with Georgia Sauce. Close lid. Every 10 minutes, baste chicken and turn over. Chicken is done in 45 minutes to 1 hour of total cooking time. Serve immediately with reserved hot Georgia Sauce.

Serves 3 or 4.

Pasta salads marry well with dishes featuring tomato-based sauces. Pair Sweet-Sour Macaroni Salad with Georgia Chicken for a meal fit for a barbecue at Tara.

Bring a wonder of Tarheel cooking to your backyard by duplicating a favorite family-style menu from Parker's, of Wilson, North Carolina.

A NORTH CAROLINA BARBECUE

Pit-Roasted Pork Shoulder

New Brunswick Stew

Corn Sticks

Parker's Coleslaw

Barbecue Potatoes

Bread Pudding With Brandy Sauce

Beverage Suggestion: Iced Sun Tea

Even within the state of North Carolina, there are different styles of barbecue. Those in the western part of the state use a tomato-based sauce; those in the eastern section proudly boast that their vinegar-based sauce is the only way to do barbecue. Some say the best barbecue in eastern Carolina is the one you'll find at historic Parker's Barbecue in Wilson, North Carolina. This menu replicates their popular family-style dinner, an all-you-can-eat feast. It's a classic stick-to-the-ribs example of hearty southern cooking at its finest. Recipes serve 8 to 10.

PREPARATION PLAN

Most of this menu can be prepared a day or so in advance of your party. New Brunswick Stew is famous, in fact, for the ability to grow in flavor after several days in the refrigerator. It's so durable in fact, that you might make it up and freeze it for use at your convenience. Coleslaw can be prepared the day before you plan to eat it, just wrap it well, refrigerate, and stir before serving. The pork shoulder can be cooked the day before—or at least a few hours before—your party. Reheat the pork in a non-aluminum pan, tightly covered, in a 325° F oven for 30 to 45 minutes. Corn Sticks can be baked the day before; finish off the deep frying right before serving. Start the potatoes an hour before serving. Make the Bread Pudding dessert the day before and reheat it in the oven. Mix up the Brandy Sauce after your main meal.

ICED SUN TEA

Drinking tea is just about synonymous with being in North Carolina. Nothing quite hits the spot like cold tea at the end of a hot summer day. Don't bother heating up the kitchen with a kettle full of boiling water when the sun can easily make your tea for you.

> 2 *bags black tea*
> 1 *bag mint tea*
>   *Ice cubes*
>   *Sugar, to taste*
>   *Lemon slices, for garnish*
>   *Mint leaves, for garnish*

1. Fill a 1½-gallon glass jar with tap water. Submerge tea bags in the water and cover with a lid. Place in a sunny location. Be sure to pick a spot where pets and children will not turn over the tea accidentally.

2. Allow tea to steep until desired strength is obtained (4 to 6 hours). Discard tea bags, add ice cubes, and place jar in the refrigerator to chill (about 1 hour).

3. Add sugar. Serve very cold over ice in a tall glass garnished with lemon slices and mint leaves.

Makes 1 gallon.

PIT-ROASTED PORK SHOULDER

Allow 6 to 8 hours for the shoulder to cook. The success of this recipe depends on maintaining an even temperature of 225° F inside the barbecue grill. This allows the roast to tenderize and remain moist as it slowly cooks. The finished meat will literally fall off the bone.

> 1 *fresh pork shoulder (5 to 7 lb)*
> 1⅓ *cups cider vinegar*
> 2 *tablespoons crushed red pepper, or to taste*
> 1 *tablespoon salt, or to taste*
> 1 *cup North Carolina Sauce (see page 80)*

1. Prepare fire for the indirect-heat method of cooking (see page 12). When fire is ready, place pork shoulder on grill, skin side up. Close vents until achieving a steady temperature of 225° F. Use an instant-read thermometer to monitor the temperature during cooking and add more coals as needed. Pork is done when meat shreds easily with a fork inserted next to the bone (after 6 to 8 hours of cooking time).

2. Remove outer skin (cracklings). Pull meat away from bone, and coarsely chop with a large knife. If desired, mix in a handful of chopped cracklings.

3. Place meat in mixing bowl and add vinegar, red pepper, and salt. Mix well and taste for seasoning. Add more red pepper or salt as needed. Serve immediately with North Carolina Barbecue Sauce. Mixture can be covered and refrigerated at this point and reheated later.

Serves 8 to 10.

NEW BRUNSWICK STEW

This dish originated in Brunswick, Georgia, and the first versions used squirrel meat. Parker's uses chicken in combination with canned vegetables and butter beans. Don't be scared off by the canned vegetables. Slowly simmered for 2 to 3 hours, this stew will satisfy any gourmet. If you can't find dried butter beans, substitute dried baby lima beans.

- 1 pound dried butter beans
- 2 chickens (about 3½ lb each), quartered
- 2 cans (14 oz each) tomato purée
- 1 can (17 oz) creamed corn
- 1 can (17 oz) cut green beans
- 1 tablespoon paprika
  Salt and pepper, to taste

1. The night before cooking, wash butter beans in cold water and place in a large saucepan. Cover with 2 quarts cold water. The next morning, simmer beans for 2 to 3 hours until tender. Reserve.

2. Wash chickens and place in large stockpot. Cover with water and bring to a boil. Skim surface of water to remove debris, and reduce heat to a slow simmer. Cook until chicken falls off the bone (about 45 minutes). Drain chickens and reserve stock. When chickens are cool enough to handle, separate meat from bones and skin. Discard skin and reserve meat. Place bones back in stock and continue to slowly boil for an additional 30 minutes.

3. In a large non-aluminum saucepan, combine cooked butter beans, chicken meat, tomato purée, corn, green beans, paprika, and 8 cups of reserved chicken stock. Slowly simmer 2 to 3 hours, stirring frequently to prevent burning. Season with salt and pepper. Add more stock if necessary during cooking. Stew should be thick and savory. Chicken meat will fall apart into threads and spread throughout stew.

Serves 8 to 10.

CORN STICKS

This dish is an interesting version of traditional hush puppies. Instead of dropping corn batter into hot oil, Parker's bakes it until barely done in cast-iron molds in a huge oven with rotating shelves. They are then finished off in hot oil. The secret to this dish is the quality of the cornmeal—try to find the freshest available.

- 1 cup fine-grind cornmeal
- 1 cup coarse-grind cornmeal
- 1¼ cups (approximately) water
- 8 tablespoons butter, melted
- 1 teaspoon salt
  Oil, for molds and frying

1. Preheat oven to 500° F. In a large mixing bowl, combine cornmeals, water, butter, and salt. The amount of water required will vary according to the quality of the cornmeal. Batter should be thick, and fall slowly from a raised wooden spoon.

2. Lightly oil cast-iron corn-stick molds. Use any shape of mold as long as the depth is about ½ to 1 inch. Fill molds and place in hot oven. Corn sticks are done baking when they just start to turn light gold (10 to 15 minutes). Remove from molds and cool on wire racks.

3. Heat oil in deep skillet to about 375° F. Carefully drop baked corn sticks into oil, 6 to 8 at a time. Turn over several times with tongs and remove when dark golden brown. Keep warm in oven until all sticks are cooked. Serve immediately.

Makes 24 to 30 corn sticks.

PARKER'S COLESLAW

Everyone has their own version of coleslaw. At Parker's the slaw has a distinctive mustard flavor. You can make this the day before to save time.

- 2 cabbages (2½ to 3 lb total)
- ⅓ cup mustard
- ⅓ cup white vinegar
- ⅓ cup sugar
- ⅓ cup mayonnaise
  Sprinkle of celery seed

Shred cabbages with a large knife or in a food processor. In a large bowl mix mustard, vinegar, sugar, mayonnaise, and celery seed. Add cabbage and toss well. Refrigerate covered for at least 1 hour before serving.

Serves 8 to 10.

BARBECUE POTATOES

When people see these potatoes piled high in bowls on the table at Parker's, they think they are barbecued. Actually, they are boiled in water colored by paprika, which gives them a reddish color.

- 10 pounds potatoes, peeled and quartered
- 2 tablespoons paprika
  Salt and pepper, to taste
- ½ cup barbecue drippings (optional)

Place potatoes in a large stockpot and cover with cold water. Add paprika, salt and pepper, and (if desired) barbecue drippings. Bring to a boil and simmer slowly until tender, about 30 minutes. Remove potatoes from pan, dot with butter and a splash of cooking liquid and serve.

Serves 8 to 10.

BREAD PUDDING WITH BRANDY SAUCE

Reheat bread pudding in a 325° F oven while making the Brandy Sauce.

- 3 cups milk
- 4 large eggs
- 1 cup sugar
- 1 teaspoon vanilla extract
- 2 teaspoons cinnamon
- 1 teaspoon nutmeg
- ¼ teaspoon allspice
- ½ teaspoon salt
- ¼ cup butter, melted
- 1 loaf day-old French bread
- ⅔ cup raisins

Brandy Sauce

- 3 large eggs
- ⅓ cup sugar
- ½ teaspoon vanilla extract
- ¼ cup butter, melted
- ¼ cup brandy
- ½ cup milk
- ⅛ teaspoon cloves

1. In a heavy saucepan, scald milk. Remove from heat and allow to cool to room temperature. In a separate bowl mix eggs, sugar, vanilla, cinnamon, nutmeg, allspice, salt, and butter. When milk is cool, whisk into egg mixture. Do not overmix.

2. Preheat oven to 350° F. Cut bread into 2-inch cubes. Place bread and raisins in bottom of a 3- to 4-quart earthenware or glass casserole dish. Cover with egg-milk mixture. Bake uncovered until a toothpick placed in center comes out clean and top begins to brown (about 1 hour). Refrigerate and reheat if desired. Serve warm or at room temperature with Brandy Sauce.

Serves 6 to 8.

Brandy Sauce In a heavy saucepan whisk eggs until thoroughly mixed. Whisk in sugar, vanilla, and melted butter. Cook over low heat, stirring often, until mixture begins to thicken (6 to 8 minutes). Remove from heat and stir in brandy, milk, and cloves. Beat with electric mixer for several minutes, until sauce resembles heavy cream. Serve warm.

Makes 1 cup.

... ABOUT PARKER'S

In the days before golden arches dotted the American highway, roadhouses were an essential part of the culinary landscape. Not only did locals frequent these restaurants, but weary travelers stopped as well. In the South, barbecue joints were by far the most prevalent type of roadhouse. Before Interstate 95 cut through North Carolina, Highway 301 served as the major north-south corridor for the New York–Florida traffic. So when brothers Ralph and Graham Parker decided to open a roadhouse restaurant with their childhood friend Henry Brewer, the southern outskirt of Wilson, right off Highway 301, was the obvious choice.

Parker's classic barbecue house was founded in 1946 and has been an institution ever since. Although it started modestly with one main dining room and a backdoor takeout, it wasn't long before people discovered the magic of those pit-roasted pigs. Local workers soon appeared in the morning to buy lunch at the takeout counter, which was often busier than the main restaurant. Building addition after addition onto the original house, Parker's can now accommodate 350 people. The menu has always focused on the family-style dinner barbecue featured on these pages.

In one week at Parker's, the staff cooks more than 100 pigs and 2,000 chickens for a very loyal clientele. Originally Parker's cooked split pigs over logs slowly smoldering in pits dug in the ground. Now the split pigs lie on metal grates that are positioned between gas grills that are below and above. As the pigs cook slowly (at about 225° F), juices drip from the meat and vaporize on the hot lava rocks. Rather than relying on hardwood chips to produce smoke and flavor, the pork depends only on the smoke that its juices produce naturally. The result is meat imbued with a distinctive smoky flavor.

In six to eight hours, the pork becomes so tender that it falls off the bone. At this point the pigs are removed from the "pits," and the meat is pulled off and coarsely chopped. Some of the cracklings (pork skin) are also chopped and mixed with the meat for added flavor. Parker's then adds the finishing touch: a mixture of cider vinegar, crushed red pepper, salt, and pan drippings. This barbecue is the essence of simplicity, and it is delicious.

This feast can be rendered using a pork shoulder instead of a split pig. But be careful: Word of your mastery of barbecue may spread fast among your friends, causing you to repeat this feast time and time again.

Open from 9 a.m. to 9 p.m. seven days a week, with a strong emphasis on instant service, Parker's was way ahead of the fast-food craze. When you seat yourself before one of the long picnic-style tables that along with gingham curtains make up the decor at Parker's, it is only minutes before the plates of food arrive to crowd your table.

Over the years many stories have developed about this North Carolina institution. One includes Ralston Purina's opening of a huge feed plant in the early sixties in Wilson. On the christening day the company threw a giant party for nearly 20,000 people. Minnie Pearl and other country-western stars entertained. Parker's fed them all. Another story claims that locals at Parker's occasionally spot a barefoot Andy Griffith at the takeout window, picking up lunch to relish at his nearby summer home.

In the summer of 1987 founding partner Henry Brewer died, leaving semiretired partners Ralph and Graham Parker to ponder the fate of the restaurant. It didn't take them long to decide to keep Parker's going; it continues to be run by a loyal and dedicated staff.

So the next time you're passing through Wilson, North Carolina, pull off the highway and enter another time—a time for good food and good people at a classic roadhouse.

A few easy tricks make cooking over a campfire no more difficult than using your range at home. Bring plenty of supplies in case the fish aren't biting.

Campfire Cooking

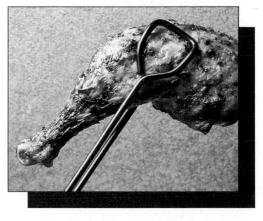

Cooking over a campfire, a part of everyday life just a few generations ago, can throw the most experienced modern cook off stride. Faced with the unfamiliar tasks of gathering wood and turning out a full meal over a smoky fire, campfire cooks could possibly forget that camping is supposed to be fun. The first rule of campfire cooking is to do as much pretrip preparation as possible. Learning to cook over a fire can take some practice, so start with basic recipes—everyone knows that even simple foods taste great out-of-doors. Recipes in this chapter are easy yet so elegant that your camping companions may forget that they're supposed to be roughing it.

CAMPFIRE COOKING TAKES PLANNING

Paying attention to details ahead of time will make your camp cooking—and your whole camping experience—easier and more fun. Your camping style is, of course, the major factor in the type of campfire cooking you'll be doing, the amount of food you'll bring, and how you'll need to pack it. Hikers and backpackers must be constantly aware of weight and bulk when planning menus and packing food and equipment. Campground campers or "car campers" have fewer restrictions but should try and minimize the number of items.

When packing for camping have on hand sealable plastic bags (both quart and gallon sizes), a ballpoint or indelible marking pen (other types may smear and become illegible if they get wet), and a roll of self-adhesive labels for identifying the food and the meal it's for. Include cooking instructions on the label if necessary. If you label all containers, you won't have to open them until it's time to use those ingredients. Prewritten instructions will help you to stay organized and allow you to delegate some cooking jobs in camp.

Take foods that don't take up much room—especially valuable cooler space. You can shop at outdoor-equipment stores for backpacking food that doesn't need refrigeration. Some types of freeze-dried foods leave much to be desired, but some are fine; experiment with different brands before you take them on the road. If plenty of water will be available at your campsite, consider bringing powdered juice mixes instead of large containers of drinks. If you will be away from refrigeration, take along powdered milk to supplement your milk supply.

Because space is a concern, it's a good idea to repackage some food. Transfer bulk food to containers that are smaller, more efficient, unbreakable, and leakproof. Remember to always label anything you repackage. The plastic containers that film is sold in are useful for carrying spices, fresh herbs, and small loose items such as matches.

Outdoor-equipment stores and mail-order firms (see page 121) carry backpacking supplies that can help you pack food efficiently. Look for plastic food tubes that can be filled and sealed from the bottom. These are good for transporting peanut butter, mustard, honey, and jellies. They are especially helpful on a day hike where you'll be preparing lunch away from camp.

Plastic bottles especially designed for camping (Nalgene is a common brand) come in all sizes and are wonderful for carrying liquids because they don't leak after you give the lid an extra twist. Keep in mind that oils are especially apt to leakage so give the lid of oil containers an extra twist, then enclose the entire bottle in a sealable plastic bag for leakage insurance.

The best way to carry eggs is to break them into a Nalgene-type bottle (leave yolks whole and unbeaten until you're ready to use them). By breaking them beforehand you avoid having messy broken eggs in the camp cooler and shells adding to the garbage.

When planning preparation at home, begin by laying out a chart with the number of days and the meals to be served each day, and then list the foods to take along.

When planning menus always think about ease of preparation in camp. Prepare one-pot meals in your home kitchen, seal them into a plastic container, and simply heat them in a pot on the campfire for dinner the first night. Wash and cut all vegetables and salad ingredients at home, and store them in plastic bags in your camp cooler until needed. Mix dry ingredients for recipes such as Steamed Corn Bread (see page 118) at home, and put the mix into a bag.

Don't forget to affix a label onto all bags and to include instructions about use and preparation. A well-organized packing job will spare you the frustration of continually searching for things in camp.

Keeping a permanent checklist of your camping supplies, utensils, and gear can save you hours of work before a trip. If you do a lot of camping, you may want to buy a portable cupboard from one of the companies that supplies camping equipment for outfitters (see page 121) and in it keep a permanent "kitchen" complete with basic staples, spices, and cooking utensils. If you don't want to go to that expense, several heavy cardboard boxes with lids and handholds (such as those for storing business files) will do a fine job of organizing. Use a bold marking pen to label the boxes on the top and on all sides.

It's a good idea to pack together things you use at the same time. Think about the things you'll need when you first arrive in camp, for example: water containers and the equipment to get your campfire going. Pack those items together and put that box on top in your trunk. Use logic: first-used, last-packed.

If you are car camping for several days, you may want to use the system of putting meals for each day in a large plastic bag and labeling the bag with the date of use: "Wednesday, July 4." Within the large bag pack smaller bags labeled "Breakfast," "Lunch," and "Dinner." Leave the large bags in the trunk until the appropriate day.

Always know where your flashlight is. Try to bring one flashlight per person plus one for the "kitchen." It's a good idea to take a lot of matches; have a primary supply and put matches in several different places, just in case.

The most common mistake made by campers is to bring too much food. Although everyone tends to eat more when outdoors and exercising, be realistic.

The keys to a good camping trip are packing well and making some foods at home. Tomatoes, Green Onions, and Mint and Carrot-Raisin salads are shown.

The fabulous aroma of baking Double Dutch-Oven Brownies (see page 112) amidst the smells of the great outdoors is a camping experience not to be missed. In fact, plan on bringing extra ingredients for more than one batch of this wonderful campfire dessert—all your campground neighbors will want to try some. Measure all dry ingredients at home and place them in bags marked with "in camp" directions for ease of preparation when traveling.

CAMPING EQUIPMENT AND SUPPLIES

The right equipment can make a big difference in your campfire cooking experience. Although there is a wide range of equipment available from specialty suppliers, you should be able to get everything you need for cooking on a typical camping trip at the supermarket, the hardware store, and an outdoor-equipment store—without spending a great deal of money. You'll probably find that everyday items such as aluminum foil and garbage bags are more important than a fancy new cooler.

Established campgrounds may have an installed fireplace, but you may need or want to bring a rack from home. An old refrigerator or oven rack will do nicely, you could bring the rack from your home grill, or you can buy small grills from an outdoor-equipment store.

Start by getting a starter set of pots and pans for campfire cooking. You can find them in outdoor-equipment stores in stainless steel or aluminum. Stainless steel is heavier and considerably more expensive than aluminum, and often it's harder to find what you need in stainless steel because it's less popular than aluminum cookware.

You'll need at least one 3-quart pot (two are better); an 8- to 9-quart pot the smaller pot can nest in (for steaming breads); a 10- to 12-inch nonstick skillet (the kind with handles that fold over are lightweight and pack easily); and a large coffeepot. Often you can get these pots and pans as sets that nest together in a single unit and include cups, metal plates, and lids that double as skillets. (The skillets in these sets seldom have a nonstick coating, however, and you may regret not having it.) Look for pots with lids that have a snug fit, and buy pots with bail handles—the kind that can stand upright over the middle of the pot for ease in lifting off a hot fire quickly.

Pots used on a campfire will inevitably become blackened by the fire, but if you rub a coat of liquid soap on the outside of your pots and pans before you use them, they'll be easier to clean.

The long-handled cooking utensils you use for grilling at home are also good for campfire cooking; regular cooking utensils are easier to use, however, so take both the long- and short-handled versions. A hinged wire basket with a long handle works well for cooking fish, meat patties, and making toast. The nifty little Swiss Army knife is so handy you'll be using it constantly. Get the model with scissors, corkscrew, can opener, and tweezers.

Dutch ovens made of cast iron are especially good for cooking in the coals because they're thick, heavy, and distribute heat evenly. They're also relatively inexpensive; get the kind with a flat, rimmed, metal (not glass) lid for holding coals, and follow the manufacturer's directions for seasoning it before the first use.

Bring plenty of drinking water containers on your camping trip. Look for plastic collapsible containers in outdoor-equipment stores; they are inexpensive and pack into a small space. The kind with a spigot and a carrying handle with a small hole that allows you to hang it from a tree are especially handy. Two 2½-gallon containers are preferable to one 5-gallon size because carrying water will be easier and small containers tend to spring leaks less frequently. (The weight of the water probably explains why. Five gallons of water weighs 40 pounds.)

A length of plastic screen, which you can purchase from any hardware store, has many uses in camp. Put the screen over food to protect it from insects. The screen also makes a perfect "cupboard" for storing dishes after they're washed (see photograph page 96). Put the screen on the clothesline, folded in half lengthwise with the fold down, and fasten the two edges together and onto the clothesline with clothespins. This makes a long, open tube. Put dishes in either end; they dry quickly in their open-air cupboard and are fairly well protected from insects as well.

Plastic garbage bags also have a number of uses. If it rains, they can be used for covering up gear and firewood. Cut holes for head and arms, and you have an emergency rain poncho. The 13-gallon size works nicely as a container for a big green salad. People have even been known to enjoy a hot bath in the heavy-duty, 30-gallon size. Just let the water heat up inside a black bag by setting it in the sun for a few hours.

Bring a roll of heavy-duty aluminum foil. You'll use it for cooking vegetables on the grill and in the coals, to make a tight seal for your pot when you steam breads, to heat up bread, as a makeshift plate, as a warming pan, and more. Don't forget the aluminum foil. It may well be the most indispensible item on your list.

Most campgrounds have large picnic tables, but you may very well camp in a place where there are no tables. There are several kinds of portable tables on the market. The compact roll-up table with screw-in legs is fairly sturdy and easy to transport. If you need to bring a table, don't forget to bring chairs!

Coolers, or ice chests, can keep food refrigerated for days. The cooler is kept cold with ice cubes, block ice, "blue ice," or ice that has been frozen in plastic bottles, milk cartons, or other containers. Blocks of ice and "blue ice" last far longer than do loose ice cubes.

Styrofoam camping coolers are inexpensive, but they are rather flimsy. They will do the job, but it seems that—inevitably—someone sits on the cooler and breaks it!

Metal coolers are heavily insulated, and will keep food colder and longer than foam or even the heavyweight plastic coolers. Metal coolers are the best and the most expensive.

Plastic coolers will keep food cold long enough for most camping trips, however. An excellent style features plastic bottles that screw into the inside of the lid. Freeze water in the bottles at home. Once affixed to the lid, they don't take up valuable space like block ice, and they don't make the melting mess that exposed ice does.

Keep all perishable food in your camp cooler. To slow bacteria growth you must maintain the cooler at a temperature of 45° F or below. Open your camp cooler as few times as possible and do not leave it standing open. Try to keep your cooler in a shady area. Remove food from the cooler only when you are ready to serve it.

CAMP STOVES

Although the recipes in this chapter were designed to be cooked over an open fire, you may find times when you need to use a camp stove on a camping trip. The chance of rain is, of course, a major consideration in planning to bring along a camp stove. The lack of rain, which often results in a ban on open fires, is another reason to bring a stove. If you are camping in an area where gathering wood is prohibited, you may want to bring in a camp stove rather than carry in wood and charcoal briquettes. Or you may simply want to use the campfire as a supplement to the camp stove.

Be sure to check with local authorities about the availability of wood for cooking when making your camping reservations.

First, decide how large you want your stove to be and what kind of fuel you prefer. For car camping you could get a large stove with several burners, or one or two small one-burner backpacking stoves. Primary fuel choices are butane, propane, and white gas. Butane and propane stoves have fuel cartridges and usually are the easiest to light, but they can be finicky at high altitudes or on very cold mornings. Even though it takes a little practice to learn to light a white-gas stove, many experienced camp cooks prefer them because white gas burns hotter and more efficiently than propane and butane. Moreover, finding the fuel cartridge that fits your particular butane or propane stove can be a problem, but white gas is readily available at camping supply stores and gasoline stations throughout the United States and Canada.

CAMPING EQUIPMENT CHECKLIST

You may not need every one of the items on this checklist of equipment every time you go camping. This equipment is enough to cook most meals, including those in the dinner and brunch menus that begin on page 111. Most of this equipment is found in home kitchens, and your regular equipment and utensils can, of course, double as your camping equipment. The problems of not having two sets are that you must pack up your outdoor kitchen every time you plan a trip and that your gear will suffer from use over an open fire.

It's really not necessary to bring an axe if you're gathering wood around the campsite. In fact, if you find you have to use an axe to get enough wood for your campfire, then wood is so scarce that it's ecologically unsound to gather wood for cooking (forests need down wood to make soil in which to continue to grow). Do not assume there will be plenty of wood for a campfire. Bring wood and charcoal briquettes from home or use a camp stove.

If you use an axe to split wood, be aware that a long-handled axe is safer than a short-handled axe: If you miss your target with a long-handled axe, the blade is likely to bite harmlessly into the ground. The arc that a short-handled axe travels is a path that is liable to stop at your knee or shin. So, be careful when chopping wood. Although a first aid kit is recommended, the hope is that you won't need it.

Campfire Equipment

Water bottle with sprayer, for flare-ups
Grilling rack
Bucket
Shovel
Long-handled axe
Wooden kitchen matches
Newspaper (to help start fire)
Fire starter, such as a candle (optional)
Oven mitts and hot pads
Matches

Cooking Equipment

2 three-quart pots
1 eight-quart pot
1 ten- or twelve-inch nonstick skillet
1 nine- to twenty-cup coffeepot
1 four-quart Dutch oven (optional)
2 large metal spoons, with long handles
2 spatulas, with long handles
2 meat forks, one with a long handle
Wooden spoons
1 long-handled wire-basket grill (optional)
Large tongs
Sharp knife
Swiss Army–style knife, or be sure to include can opener, corkscrew, scissors, and paring knife
Popcorn basket (optional)

Miscellaneous Equipment

Cooler
Water containers
Cutting board
Cheese grater
Strainer (for coffee grounds if you don't use filters)
Measuring cup
Measuring spoons
Nalgene-type plastic bottles
Plastic food tubes
Flashlight
Clothespins
Clothesline
Plastic screen (about 3 by 6 feet)
Paper towels
Dish towels
Presoaped scrub sponge
Biodegradable soap
Plastic dishpan
Aluminum foil, heavy-duty
Garbage bags, both 30-gallon and 10-gallon sizes
Sealable plastic bags, several sizes
Roll-up table (optional)
Camp stove, fuel, funnel (optional)
First-aid kit
Pump or water purifier
Insect repellent
Sunscreen
Toilet paper
Safety pins and rubber bands
Sewing kit

Serving Equipment

Tablecloth, oilcloth is best
1 insulated cup per person
1 dinner-sized plate per person
1 flatwear set per person
Paper napkins
Paper cups

First-aid Kit

A good first-aid kit is essential on a camping trip. You should also have a book on first aid. *Medicine for the Outdoors* by Paul S. Auerbach, M.D. (Little, Brown and Company), is excellent. *Mountaineering Medicine, A Wilderness Medical Guide* by Fred T. Darvill, Jr., M.D. (Seattle Mountaineers), is useful as well as small enough to fit into a first aid kit. Put together a kit of the basic supplies listed below and hope you won't need to open it. Don't forget to bring any prescription medicines members of your camping party may need.

Assorted plastic bandages
Tape
Gauze
Elastic bandage
Tweezers
Scissors
Needle
Soap
Paper and pencil
Aspirin
Upset stomach remedy
Hydrocortisone cream
Antiseptic cream
Snakebite kit
Blister kit (especially if hiking)
Telephone number of nearest hospital
Telephone number of family doctor

Emergency Equipment

Equip yourself properly for any emergency. In most areas it's against the law to have an open fire without a bucket and shovel nearby, and it is an excellent idea in all cases. The United States Forest Service recommends that you keep a full bucket of water next to your campfire at all times. A garden shovel from home is fine, though shorter-handled camping shovels are easier to use.

Gathering Wood

Firewood is often scarce, and wood gathering is banned in many areas. Check with local authorities about wood gathering and fire laws before you set up camp. You may not be allowed to have an open fire at all. You may need to bring charcoal briquettes or wood. If wood gathering is allowed, here are some tips on what to look for and what to avoid.

First, take wood only from the ground. Do not chop down trees or break off branches from standing trees. Avoid green wood; take dry wood that breaks easily. The kind of wood available is largely determined by where you are. If you have a choice, however, remember that hardwoods (oak, beech, madrone) make the best coals, and light woods such as pine and fir are best for starting a fire.

Wood that seems very lightweight is probably rotten. If it burns at all, it won't burn well. The thick bark of a large fallen fir can make good coals, but it depends on how long the tree has been down; it takes a hot, well-established fire to light the bark.

Gather wood in graduated sizes. You'll need tiny dry twigs to start your fire, kindling to get it going, and larger sticks and logs to make good coals. Break the wood in sizes to accommodate your fireplace, and stack in bundles according to size at a convenient yet safe distance from the fire.

Don't gather more wood than you need. Keep your fire small. A small fire gives plenty of heat for cooking. Native Americans used to say that the white man built a big fire and kept himself warm by running around gathering wood; the Indian built a small fire and kept warm by the fire. Build an Indian fire.

. . . FOR SAFE CAMPFIRE COOKING

When you build a campfire, you're creating something beautiful, useful, and spiritually satisfying—and you're taking on a responsibility. An unattended campfire or sparks from too large a fire can cause an entire forest to burn. Make your campfire safe.

Make sure your fire is legal. Find out where and under what conditions you can legally build a fire. Permits are often required and are available at no charge from the local Forest Service office.

Established campgrounds usually provide fire pits, and it can be illegal to build fires anywhere but in the provided fireplaces.

Build your campfire away from overhanging branches, steep slopes, logs, and dry grass and leaves. Scrape away litter, duff, and any burnable material in a 10-foot circle around the fire. This will act as a firebreak if any embers jump from your fire.

Make sure your fire isn't too close to the rest of your gear. Sparks burn annoying holes in nylon tents and sleeping bags.

Be sure to dig below the duff and into the mineral soil to build your fire ring (see page 104).

Make sure your camping group—especially children—are aware of the placement of the fire In addition, everyone should know the location of the water bottle and bucket for extinguishing the fire and be aware of fire safety procedures.

Any time you leave your camp, make sure your campfire is completely out. Drown it with water. Make sure all coals and sticks are wet. Check for burning embers under surrounding rocks. Stir the ashes, add more water, and stir again. Touch all sticks and charred material and be sure everything has been extinguished and cooled.

Don't Feed The Animals

Given the slightest opportunity, bears, raccoons, and varmints will raid your food supply. Just because you don't see any animals, don't assume that they're not around. Most of these raiders are nocturnal, and they are unbelievably clever—especially bears. Bears can recognize a camping cooler through the window of your car. Stories about Yellowstone National Park tell of bears that have learned that they can pop open the doors of a closed Volkswagen by bouncing on the roof! Never underestimate the cleverness of a bear.

Probably the best way to protect your food when car camping is to put it in the trunk of your car, out of sight. If you're in an area where bears are a real problem, also put away toothpaste, cosmetics, soap, and other substances that are "humanly" fragrant. If you're camping away from your car, "bear boxes," metal boxes with metal clasps that bears can't manipulate, are sometimes provided. Also try hanging food on steel cables (they are often provided in established campgrounds), or from a tree using a counterbalance method to keep it safe. Ask the local rangers how to hang your food in a tree using the counterbalance method. They can usually tell you whether there are problems with animals and have pamphlets with instructions about how to keep your food safe. Follow the instructions to the letter. Don't let the account of your trip be another legend of a ruined excursion caused by lost food.

Observe and enjoy the wildlife at a safe distance. Do not leave food out for animals or feed them. Keep in mind that when you protect your food, you're not only doing yourself a favor, you're also showing respect for wild animals by preventing them from becoming marauding pests.

BUILDING A FIREPLACE

If fireplaces are not provided in your campground, you can build one—or you can improve an existing fireplace by rearranging the stones. The size and type of fireplace you need will depend on what you're cooking, how you're cooking it, and the size of your group. Build a fire large enough for your needs, but no more. Your fireplace can be a simple trench, a fire ring, or an elaborate keyhole fireplace. Recipes in this chapter were developed for use on a keyhole fireplace.

Trench Fireplace

To build a trench fireplace, you'll need to clear an area for your fire ring. Then, find four large, flat rocks. Dig a shallow trench in mineral soil, the layer below the organic soil. (Organic soil can burn and cause a fire to spread.) Make the trench about 2 feet long and narrower than the width of your grill rack. Leave the trench open at both ends to allow good air circulation, which will keep the fire burning efficiently. Place a rock on each side of the trench and balance the grill rack on top of the rocks, making sure the rack is stable. This fireplace is good for cooking simple meals for small groups, it can be built quickly, and it is easily dismantled. It's the best fireplace for "low-impact camping."

Fire Ring

A fire ring is the classic campfire. Whenever possible use an established fire ring rather than building a new one. You do a service to the area by cleaning up a ruined fire ring and you'll make less of an impact on the environment. Make sure you place your fire ring on bare ground and that it is at least 100 feet back from your water source.

Start by clearing dead leaves and loose forest litter 10 feet back from where you want your fire. Then dig a shallow circular fireplace; you need to dig through the duff (the topsoil containing flammable organic material) and slightly down into the mineral soil. Next surround the fireplace with a shallow trench also dug down into the mineral soil. The moat will act as a firebreak, keeping sparks from the campfire from igniting the organic soil.

Now surround the fireplace circle with large rocks. Place the grill rack on top of the rocks, making sure the grill rack will be stable enough to hod several cooking pots. Use this fireplace for cooking and then remove the grill rack for after-dinner campfire watching.

Keyhole Fireplace

The keyhole fireplace is actually two fires, one for warming campers and baking food in the coals and a smaller fire to cook on that uses coals from the large fire. It's shaped like a keyhole and is an efficient arrangement for all campfire cooking methods. Clear an area as for a fire ring. Gather flat rocks and take care fitting them together. The round part of the keyhole should be large enough to accommodate the people in your group gathered around the fire, and the grill rack should fit well over the box-shaped end. Flat rocks around the fire ring that are the size of your pots and skillet can be used for keeping food warm.

Making everything solid and level is one of the most important things to keep in mind when building a fireplace. Cooking on a campfire is a busy job, and the cook doesn't need the dangerous distraction of balancing pots of hot food on wobbly rocks.

When you leave your camp, it's fine to leave your fireplace up if it was already established. If you built your fireplace from scratch and the campsite was previously unused, however, dismantle your fireplace. Scatter the stones and turn the black, sooty side down to the ground and out of sight. All wood should be burned to ashes. Crush remaining coals and mix them together with mineral soil. Scatter this mixture around (making sure they are completely cold first). Make the area look as if no one has been there. We are guests in the wilderness, and the idea is to camp and leave no trace.

CLEANUP

When you clean up after meals, don't put food matter or soap in streams—not even biodegradable soap. Wash dishes in a washbasin or large cooking pot, and dispose of your dishwater at least 300 feet from streams or lakes. The same rules apply for shampooing and bathing water. Use a washbasin and rinse well away from pristine water sources.

Check with the park ranger's office or other site authorities about toilet facilities and local rules concerning burying human refuse, the availability of pit toilets, or the need to bring your own portable facilities when making camping reservations.

Because so many people are using a limited area of the wilderness, burying garbage is simply not acceptable. It is a good idea to take all your garbage out of the camping area with you. Much of your garbage—vegetable peelings, discarded food, and paper items—can be burned. Be aware, however, that aluminum foil and foil packaging that looks like paper do not burn. Dispose of it with your garbage.

If you are going camping for several days, keep your garbage as clean and compact as possible. Rinse out and crush cans and other containers, and store them out of reach of animals.

When breaking camp erase all evidence that you were there. People who love the wilderness always leave a camp cleaner than they found it; they even take out garbage that others have left. Wilderness living requires a way of thinking that is different from that of our everyday lives in the city. The wilderness will remain wild and unspoiled for future generations only if protected and cared for by those who use it now.

... ABOUT WATER

Water is usually plentiful, but if you have a "dry camp," you'll need to bring water for doing dishes, putting out the campfire, cooking, drinking, and washing. The amount of drinking water you'll need depends on how active you are and on the weather. In hot weather hikers should consume a gallon of water per day. You can easily become dehydrated yet not feel thirsty, so drink lots of water when you're living outdoors—especially if you're at high elevations where the air is always very dry.

If you need to bring in your water, a good rule of thumb is to bring 2 gallons of water per person per day. Remember that the melted ice in the camp cooler is perfectly good water for many camp site cleanup chores. Be sure to check on water availability when making camping reservations and plan accordingly.

Giardia Is Not a Pasta Dish

Always make sure that there is water available at your campsite and that the water is safe to drink. If you are not sure, bring plenty of water with you for cooking and drinking. Most established campgrounds have tap water, which is perfectly safe for drinking. However, if you're getting your drinking and cooking water from a stream, lake, or spring, purify the water to protect yourself from the risk of ingesting organisms that will make you sick. *Giardia lamblia*, a parasite that inhabits the lower intestine, is of particular concern because it has become quite prevalent in the United States in the last 10 years. The symptoms, which may take from 3 days to a month to manifest, are diarrhea, stomach cramps, flatulence, and sometimes vomiting. If you experience these symptoms after drinking from an unusual water source, seek a doctor's care.

Water Purification

There are three ways to effectively purify water so that it is safe to drink:

1. Boil water for 5 minutes.

2. You can buy a filter pump from an outdoor-equipment store. You need at least a 0.4-micron filter to keep the giardia cysts from passing through. A popular choice among outdoor enthusiasts is the First-Need brand pump; it weighs about 12 ounces and in 1987 cost about $40. A very popular pump filter is the 23-ounce Katadyn brand. It has a 0.2-micron filter and costs about $170 in 1987.

3. Treat water with iodine. Add 10 drops (no more) of a 2-percent tincture of iodine to a quart of water and wait 30 minutes before drinking it. Don't forget to pour some of the treated water around the threads and on the lid of your water bottle so any organisms on them don't contaminate the purified water. If you add lemonade or something else to mask the taste of the iodine, don't add it until the 30 minutes have elapsed; vitamin C can counteract the action of the iodine.

There are commercial pills containing iodides that also work against giardia but they're much more expensive than a 2-percent tincture of iodine. In addition, if the pills are not used within a few weeks of opening the bottle, they begin to oxidize and become ineffective. Be warned: Bleach, halazone, pills, and other products that do not contain iodide are often sold as water purifiers, although they clean the water of some pollutants, they do not protect you against giardia.

Step-by-Step

... FOR BUILDING A FIRE AND MAKING COALS

Lighting a campfire and keeping it going is a matter of giving it enough air by using tiny dry sticks until the fire is established and then adding larger sticks at the right time. Most failed fires are a result of too much too soon. People start adding large sticks before the time is right, and the fire flickers and dies.

If you are building your fire in an established fireplace, make sure you clear away debris and burnt logs that may have been left by earlier campers. If you need to build a fireplace, see the description of different types on page 104. Before lighting any fire make sure you read the Tips for Safe Campfire Cooking on page 103.

2. *Light the tinder and keep adding dry twigs or furry sticks to the burning pile. As the fire grows, you can lay on the small pieces of wood in a teepee or log-cabin formation. The log-cabin method develops the better bed of coals.*

4. *Once the fire is really going and you want to make a bed of coals, begin laying sticks and logs parallel and touching each other. They trap the heat and make the fire burn even hotter. Large sticks and logs burn down to coals. Dense wood makes better coals than softwood. Hardwoods and sometimes thick fir or thick pine bark can make good cooking coals. A wood fire will take from 30 minutes to 1 hour to burn down sufficiently for cooking.*

1. *Start by crumpling tinder: newspapers, dry leaves, or pine needles. Then lay a pile of dry twigs (of matchstick size or smaller) or "furry sticks" on the tinder. (To make furry sticks, shave curls on the stick with a pocketknife and leave the shavings attached.)*

3. *If the fire starts to go out, blow on it. When the fire is this small, it's safe to get very close to it and blow, and often that is what it takes. Be attentive and patient, and keep adding small twigs in a crisscross pattern around the flame. Gradually add larger twigs, then sticks as the fire builds up. Keep blowing on the fire when necessary until it's well established.*

5. *Use caution when throwing loose paper, paper plates, or leaves on the fire or hot coals. A burst of wind could grab the burning paper and cause a fire. Never use lighter fluid to light wood or reignite coals. Read Campfire Cooking Methods on page 109 for information on how the coals should look before you begin cooking.*

The steaming method of campfire cooking is well demonstrated by Steamed Corn Bread (see page 118). Serve it with brunch or as a snack with milk and jam.

Dutch Oven Cowboy Eggs (see page 120), the centerpiece of the Wilderness Brunch Menu, are a light scramble of eggs and cheese. Allow campers to garnish to taste.

CAMPFIRE COOKING METHODS

In learning to cook over coals from a wood fire, nothing is more important than experience. Even the most accomplished home chef who is used to a charcoal briquette fire can make mistakes at first. Here are some tips for successful campfire cooking.

First and foremost, never underestimate the heat of a wood fire. A direct flame should be used only for boiling. Realize, though, that coals will do the job just as well and without blackening the pots. Glowing coals are really too hot for baking. Use coals for grilling meat and, if you need to bake, wait until they burn down considerably. Charcoal briquettes do a fine job of grilling, but they burn too hot to make good coals for baking anything buried in them unless they're mixed with wood coals, embers, and ashes.

Secondly, you must remember to feed the fire. It's easy to get involved in your cooking and forget that you're not at home on the range. Try to cook with the lid on pots—food will heat faster and you will save fuel.

Campfire Baking in the Coals

You need to use a Dutch oven or an aluminum foil–capped skillet to bake in the campfire coals. You can bake just about anything: beans, brownies, breads, and all sorts of desserts. The secret is to make sure the coals are not too hot. Good baking coals may seem a bit past their prime. They're mixed with ashes, and you should be able to hold your hand over them for several seconds. The fire ring is a good place to bake when the fire has been burning for a long time because there is a deep pile of coals and ashes. Bury the Dutch oven, shovel coals on the lid, and check the food often if you're in doubt. If you're using a skillet, cap it with a double or triple layer of heavy-duty aluminum foil and put coals over it. After a little practice judging the temperature of coals, you'll be turning out perfectly fine baked goods.

Campfire Steaming

Breads and cakes will be moister when steamed than when baked in the coals. They will take longer to cook, but seldom burn (unless you let the water boil away). Steaming is also a cooking method you can use on the camp stove when open fires are prohibited. Since things take quite awhile to cook when using the steam method, it's usually not a good idea to double a recipe.

You'll need two pots, one that nests inside the other with about ½ inch to spare around the edge. Oil the inside of the smaller pot, pour in the batter, and seal tightly. Place inside the larger pot. Add water to the larger pot until the surface is a couple of inches below the lip of the smaller pot. If pots are thin, use a metal plate or crumpled aluminum foil to separate them at the bottom and use both aluminum foil and the lid for a good seal. Keep the water boiling steadily for the recommended baking time. Try not to peek until the time is up, and even then you may have to cook it longer.

Buried Cooking

You can cook potatoes, yams, whole onions, sweet potatoes, and other vegetables by burying them in the coals in their jackets or wrapping them in heavy-duty aluminum foil. There is less of a chance of burning buried food than baked, but you still have to be cautious about not using glowing red coals. If you're not careful, you'll burn the vegetables. Be cautious when working near hot coals. Make sure to wear fireproof mitts and use a long-handled spoon or camping shovel to bury and uncover food.

High-Altitude Cooking

If you make your camp at 8,000 feet or higher, you'll notice that everything takes longer to cook. This is because water boils at a lower temperature when atmospheric pressure is lower. Water doesn't have to reach the sea-level boiling point of 212° F before it begins to bubble; water boils at 196.9° F at 8,000 feet, and at 194° F at 10,000 feet.

How do these facts affect specific foods? Pasta, for example, requires very hot boiling water to cook well. As a result, it's usually not a good idea to plan a dried pasta meal at high elevation (fresh pasta, however, just needs to cook a bit longer). Some cooks have moderate success with commercial dried pasta at 9,000 feet by using furiously boiling water, a high water-to-pasta ratio, and cooking it longer—but it really does turn to wallpaper paste when cooked at altitudes higher than 9,000 feet.

You'll also have trouble cooking rice, bulgur wheat, and any grains by standard methods at high altitude. Outdoor-equipment stores sell little camping pressure cookers; they really do work, and they save fuel, too.

Breads and cakes can even behave differently at 4,000 feet. You'll need to use slightly less leavening and sugar and slightly increase the liquid and flour. At 8,000 feet, increase the baking temperature by 25° F, and they will still take longer to cook. Butter pots well—cakes and breads stick more at high altitudes.

At very high elevations (9,000 to 10,000 feet), you may experience a loss of appetite, and food you usually love to eat just doesn't taste as good. Eat anyway, and drink a lot of water. Be sure to encourage children to drink water and juices when camping at high elevations. Bring packages of dried drink mixes to add to water that may not taste good to you; they also help cover the taste of water-treatment products (see page 105). Make sure you bring along soups and herb teas, which become especially appealing at high altitudes.

There's no need to scrimp on luxury just because you're dining away from home. Serve this elegant dinner menu for rave reviews on any continent.

ELEGANT CAMPING DINNER

Quick Couscous

Condiments

Dilled Cucumbers With Yogurt

Tomato, Green Onion, and Mint Salad

Camper's Lamb Curry

Pita Bread

Double Dutch-Oven Brownies

Beverage Suggestions: Mint Tea and Cabernet Sauvignon

Serving an unexpected exotic dinner on a camping trip is fun, and curry is as good on a cool evening in the mountains as it is at a summer feast on the beach. The cook can make this dinner a simple one-pot meal with bread or an elaborate presentation—the difference is in the number of condiments. This menu also enables you to follow one of the basic rules for camp cooking: Do most of the food preparation at home. The preparation instructions in the recipes tell you what to do at home and what to do in camp. All recipes serve 6.

PREPARATION PLAN

Dinner will be ready 1 to 1½ hours from the time you start the campfire, although there are only 30 minutes of actual food preparation. Add another 40 minutes to make the tea and brownies after dinner. Once you start the campfire, assemble all ingredients and cooking equipment. After the fire has burned down to a low flame or to very hot coals (about ½ hour), put the curry on the grill to heat. Make sure the fire under it isn't too hot, and stir the curry often. Put foil-wrapped purchased pita bread on the grill over coals producing medium-low heat. Turn it often. When the curry has warmed through, put the water for Quick Couscous over heat to boil. Set out the condiments and salads in individual bowls on the camp "salad bar." Add the Quick Couscous to the boiling water and in five minutes, dinner is served. After dinner, while the coals are burning low, prepare the brownies. Boil the water and brew the tea while the brownies are cooking.

QUICK COUSCOUS

Couscous is a grainlike pasta made from durum wheat. It is the national dish of the Maghreb people of Morocco, Algeria, and Tunisia and is sometimes called Moroccan pasta. It can be used in place of rice and is delicious and supereasy to prepare. Make sure you get the quick-cooking, medium-grain type.

> 2 cups water
> 2 tablespoons butter, optional
> ½ teaspoon salt, optional
> 2 cups couscous

In camp:
Bring the water to a boil with butter and salt, if desired. Stir in couscous, cover, remove from heat, and let rest for 5 minutes. Fluff with a fork and serve with Camper's Lamb Curry.

Serves 6.

CONDIMENTS

You only need a little taste of each condiment, and you can bring them all or only a few. Most curry lovers feel that chutney is a must though.

> *Chutney*
> 2 *to 3 eggs, hard-cooked, peeled, and chopped*
> *Ginger preserves*
> *Sweet pickles*
> ½ *cup raisins*
> ⅓ *cup shelled and chopped peanuts*
> ⅓ *cup unsweetened dried coconut*
> 1 *or 2 bananas, peeled and sliced*
> 1 *or 2 kiwifruit, peeled and sliced*

In camp:
In individual bowls, set out chutney, eggs, preserves, pickles, raisins, peanuts, coconut, bananas (bananas will cool down a hot mouth), and kiwifruit. Let diners spoon each onto Camper's Lamb Curry and Quick Couscous as desired.

Serves 6.

DILLED CUCUMBERS WITH YOGURT

These fresh-tasting cucumbers are something of a cross between a salad and a condiment to use with the curried lamb.

> 2 *to 3 cucumbers*
> ⅔ *cup plain yogurt*
> ½ *teaspoon dill weed*

At home:
Peel and thinly slice cucumbers and mix with yogurt and dill. Pack in tightly sealed plastic container. Salad is most flavorful if ingredients are allowed to meld for a few hours, but is best used within 24 hours.

In camp:
Serve in individual bowls.

Serves 6.

TOMATO, GREEN ONION, AND MINT SALAD

3 large tomatoes
3 green onions
4 to 5 sprigs fresh mint

At home:
Dice tomatoes, mince green onions and mint, and mix together. Pack in tightly sealed plastic container. Salad is most flavorful if ingredients are allowed to meld for a few hours but is best used within 24 hours.

In camp:
Serve in individual bowls.

Serves 6.

CAMPER'S LAMB CURRY

Curry is a movable feast—it travels well—and the garlic, ginger, and spices are natural preservatives. For full flavor this curry should be prepared at least 24 hours in advance, and you can prepare it days ahead if you freeze it. Just make sure it's thawed in time for dinner.

1¼ cups plain yogurt
¼ teaspoon crushed red pepper flakes, or to taste
½ to 1 teaspoon salt
3 pounds boneless lamb stew meat, cut in 1-inch cubes
¼ cup ghee (see Note)
2 cups chopped onion
1 to 2 tablespoons finely chopped fresh ginger
3 to 5 large cloves garlic, minced
2 teaspoons crushed coriander seed
1 teaspoon each ground turmeric and crushed cumin seed
½ teaspoon ground cinnamon
⅛ teaspoon crushed cardamom seed
1 to 2 tablespoons vindaloo paste (hottest) or curry paste (optional, see Note)
1 cup chicken broth
Onion rings, for garnish
Lemon wedges, for garnish

At home:
1. In a large mixing bowl, combine 1 cup of the yogurt, pepper flakes, salt, and lamb. Mix well, cover, and place in refrigerator. Let marinate for 3 to 12 hours, stirring occasionally.

2. In a large pot over medium-high heat, melt ghee. Stir in chopped onion, ginger, garlic, coriander, turmeric, cumin, cinnamon, cardamom, and vindaloo paste. Cook over medium-high heat until onion is tender (about 7 minutes).

3. Stir yogurt and lamb mixture into ghee mixture. Slowly blend chicken broth into remaining yogurt, and then add to curry mixture. Bring to a boil, reduce heat, cover, and simmer until meat is tender, 1½ to 2 hours. Refrigerate for up to 3 days or freeze.

In camp:
Heat curry in a large pot over coals producing medium heat, taking care to stir often. Serve over Quick Couscous and garnish with onion rings and lemon wedges.

Serves 6.

Note Ghee is also known as clarified butter. Vindaloo and curry pastes are available at Indian groceries.

DOUBLE DUTCH-OVEN BROWNIES

Smelling brownies cooking in the midst of the glorious smells of the great outdoors is an experience long remembered. You can, of course, bake them in a home oven at 350° F for 30 minutes using a Dutch oven or 9-inch square pan.

½ cup slivered almonds
3 tablespoons amaretto or water
Scant ½ cup sugar
¾ cup unsifted flour
¼ teaspoon baking soda
¼ teaspoon salt
1 package (12 oz) semisweet chocolate chips
¼ teaspoon almond extract
2 tablespoons butter, plus butter for preparing pan
2 eggs, slightly beaten

At home:
Toast almonds in a small dry pan until light brown. When almonds are cool put them in a food processor or blender and chop. Put almonds in a small plastic bag and include finely chopped nuts and nut powder. Put amaretto, if used, in a small Nalgene-type plastic bottle. Measure sugar and put it in a separate plastic bag. In a medium bowl mix flour, baking soda, and salt; put mixture in a plastic bag. Include the package of chocolate chips in your brownie kit, too. Enclose bags and bottle of almond extract in a gallon-sized sealable plastic bag and affix label with cooking instructions.

In camp:
1. After dinner, while coals are burning low, put sugar, amaretto, and the 2 tablespoons butter in 3-quart pot and stir over low heat until mixture boils. Add about half the chocolate chips, remove from heat, and stir until blended. Add eggs and almond extract and keep stirring.

2. Add flour mixture to sugar mixture and stir until blended. Add the rest of the chocolate chips and almonds. Pour into well-buttered 4-quart Dutch oven (10-inch diameter).

3. Nestle the Dutch oven in coals producing medium to low heat. Shovel some coals and ashes onto the lid of the Dutch oven. Brownies are done when fudgelike but not runny. It's better to cook them longer at low heat than to rush them with high heat. It should take 25 to 30 minutes for the brownies to bake, depending on how hot the coals are. If in doubt, start peeking after the first 10 minutes and look at them often, checking both the outer edge and the middle. Cut into wedges and serve hot.

Makes about 12 wedges.

Kids' Cooking

... OVER THE CAMPFIRE

It's fun and easy for a kid to make a campfire dessert. It gives you something to do after dinner, and something to eat while you sit around the fire telling ghost stories. S'mores, and Baked Apples are classic campfire foods that people have been eating for generations. The adults on your camping trip may remember eating these when they were kids. Popcorn is another great dessert for a camping trip. Make it in a special wire basket or get the kind that comes in a foil popper. Popcorn is delicious topped with melted butter, sprinkled with Parmesan cheese, or just plain. Double Dutch-Oven Brownies (see opposite page) are easy to make, and so are Banana Boats (see page 117), the camper's banana split. Ask permission from an adult before you light a campfire, and always be very careful around campfires. Be sure there's an adult there to supervise while you're cooking. Also be sure that the campfire is completely out before you leave the area.

S'MORES

These sweet treats are so delicious that after the first one you'll want "s'more." This recipe is for the classic version pictured above; you might want to try making "sophisticated s'mores" for the adults by using fancy chocolate like praline or orange liqueur and after-dinner sugar wafers instead of graham crackers.

>   1 marshmallow
>   4 chocolate candy-bar squares
>   2 graham crackers

In camp:
Toast a marshmallow on a stick over the campfire. Place chocolate on one graham cracker, top chocolate with marshmallow, and cover with second cracker to form a sandwich.

Makes 1 sandwich.

BAKED APPLES

These apples take quite a while to cook. See if one of the adults will stay in camp to watch the fire while the apples cook and you take an after-dinner hike for an hour. You will come back to a delightful dessert, which can be eaten with a spoon. If it's a little cold outside you might want to make some Mexican Hot Chocolate (see page 120) to go along with your dessert. A photograph of both of these sweet treats is also on page 120.

>   6 apples
>   1 cup raisins
>   ½ to ¾ cup firmly packed
>   brown sugar
>   4 tablespoons butter

In camp:
1. Have an adult help you core the apples. *Coring* means making a long, skinny "cup" inside each apple to hold raisins, brown sugar, and butter. Start by cutting off a shallow, round "hat" at the stem; set it aside to use later. Hollow out a space through the center of each apple, and use a knife and a teaspoon to cut out the middle of the apple. Be careful not to cut all the way through the apple.

2. In a medium bowl or pot, mix raisins and brown sugar. Put a dot of butter in each apple cup, then a spoonful of raisin mixture, and then more butter. Keep alternating until each apple is full. Replace stem cap and attach it by wrapping tightly with heavy-duty aluminum foil. Double or triple wrap each apple so the juices won't leak out.

3. Bury apples in campfire coals. Cook until soft (about 1 hour).

Serves 6.

Baked Pears Baked pears are really good, too. You'll have the most success with Bosc pears—the type that has brown, "rusty" skin. Wash each pear, cut in half lengthwise, and get an adult to help you hollow out the core. Fill the cavity of each half pear with dots of butter, brown sugar, cinnamon, and raisins. Then wrap the half pear in heavy-duty aluminum foil and bake in the coals. Pears take less time to cook than do apples (probably about 30 minutes). These pears are especially delicious with thick cream poured over them.

CLASSIC CAMPING DINNER

Carrot-Raisin Salad

Silver Chicken

Corn on the Cob

Hot Potatoes

Banana Boats

Betty's Pear Torte

Beverage Suggestions:
Camper's Coffee, Beer and
Apple Juice

This simple dinner was designed for the children on your camping trip who might not like the curry in the Elegant Camping Dinner (see page 111) or for any time basic camping fare is preferred. This entire meal can be prepared at home and warmed on the campfire, or you can actually grill the foil-wrapped chicken and bake the potatoes in the coals. The Banana Boats are a special treat that kids love to make and love to eat. Recipes serve 4 to 6.

PREPARATION PLAN

Start the campfire well ahead of dinner time. It will take a good hour for the coals to be right for baking potatoes. Allow at least 2 hours from starting the fire until you can sit down and eat the main course, although you'll be cooking just 1 to 1½ hours of that time. Add 20 minutes to cook the desserts. The salad should be prepared at home and kept chilled until serving. Once the fire is ready, gather the ingredients and utensils. When the coals are ready, bury the potatoes. Next prepare the corn for grilling. Start cooking the chicken after the potatoes are cooking well, after 20 to 30 minutes. Start the corn 20 minutes after the chicken. You may want to wait until after you've eaten to make the desserts and coffee. These desserts were designed for eating around the campfire. Although you need to be sure some of the coals have burned low before you bury the banana boats, keep some part of your fire hot enough to boil the water for coffee.

CARROT-RAISIN SALAD

This healthy, delicious salad can be prepared at home and kept in the camp cooler until dinnertime. In fact, this dish is such a universal favorite and keeps so well that you may want to remember it when designing school lunches, for picnics, or when you need a make-ahead salad for a potluck dinner.

> 4 large carrots
> ½ cup raisins
> ½ cup crushed pineapple

At home:
Scrape and coarsely grate carrots into a medium-sized mixing bowl. Add raisins and pineapple. Pack in tightly sealed plastic container and keep in cooler until served.

Serves 4 to 6.

SILVER CHICKEN

You can fry, oven bake, or barbecue this chicken at home, then wrap individual pieces in aluminum foil and let the kids warm up their own pieces on the campfire grill. Cooking foil-wrapped chicken over the campfire is easy, however, and the meat turns out moist, yet the skin is crisp on the outside. Another plus is that the chef doesn't have to be a fire fighter; Silver Chicken cooks with little flare-up from the campfire. You can use any tomato-based barbecue sauce for this dish.

> 1 frying chicken, cut up
> Salt and pepper, to taste
> Barbecue sauce of your choice
> (see page 80)

At home:
Wash chicken pieces and pat dry. Salt and pepper chicken pieces. Lightly coat each chicken piece with a favorite barbecue sauce. Individually wrap each piece in one layer of heavy-duty aluminum foil. Seal well to help prevent leakage of juices. Don't leave air space in the packet that would give chicken room to steam. Keep chicken in camp cooler.

In camp:
Cook foil-wrapped chicken for 30 to 40 minutes on a grill 6 inches above glowing coals. Turn chicken often. If you have the chicken too far from the coals or if the coals aren't hot enough, the chicken will be like steamed chicken—good but a bit bland. When done it should be crisp and brown on the outside.

Serves 4.

Even basic fare tastes great when served to those weary from hiking. Plan ahead and remember to bring plenty of food for hearty appetites.

Pile fresh corn on the grill over a blazing fire and watch the cobs steam in their own husks. Turn the Corn on the Cob frequently and be careful when removing it and other hot items from the fire. Make sure all cooks on your camping trip wear protective mitts when handling anything near the campfire or camp stove and follow the Tips for Safe Campfire Cooking (see page 103) to prevent mishaps.

CORN ON THE COB

Find the freshest corn possible for this summertime treat. You can prepare this dish by burying the corn for 30 minutes in coals producing low heat, but it's easier to cook—and not to overcook—by preparing corn on top of the grill.

> 4 ears corn, with husks
> ½ cup butter
>   Salt and pepper, to taste

In camp:
Pull back corn husks and remove silk, then close husks tightly over ears of corn. Dip in water. Place on grill over hot coals and cook, turning a quarter turn every 5 minutes, for about 20 minutes. To serve, remove from grill, remove husks, dot ears with butter, and sprinkle with salt and pepper.

Serves 4.

HOT POTATOES

If you are planning to have this menu on the first or second night out on your camping trip, you can bake your potatoes at home before the trip if you wish. After baking in a 400° F oven for about 45 minutes, allow to cool, then wrap in heavy-duty aluminum foil. It will take 10 to 15 minutes to warm them up in the coals or on top of the grill in camp. But if you plan to eat these potatoes after several days away from home you'll need to completely bake them in camp. Aside from being time consuming, it's a simple operation. At dinner serve the potatoes with all your favorite fixings. You'll want to make sure to bring along butter, sour cream, chives, cheese, salt, pepper, and whatever else you and your camping group like on potatoes. If you're planning on Hash Browns for breakfast (see page 118) the next morning, cook the potatoes you'll need for them along with the potatoes for dinner. When the extra potatoes are cooked, remove from campfire, set aside to cool, and use them the next morning.

> 4 baking potatoes

At home:
Wrap potatoes in heavy-duty aluminum foil. Through foil pierce each potato in several places with a fork.

In camp:
Bury potatoes in medium-hot coals and ashes. Keep checking to make sure that the coals are hot enough and the potatoes are actually cooking—and to be certain they're not burning. A pair of long tongs and a short-handled camp shovel work well for fishing potatoes out of the campfire. Cook until soft (about 45 minutes). Potatoes can stay warm in embers for a long time.

Serves 4.

BANANA BOATS

This dessert should be thought of as a camper's banana split. It's so delicious, you may have to make extras. If you have children on your camping trip, this dessert is easy enough for them to make on their own. These can be made at home in a low-heat oven or in your kettle-shaped covered grill as well as on the road.

    4 firm bananas
    1½ cups semisweet chocolate chips
    2 cups miniature marshmallows

In camp:

1. In each banana make a lengthwise slit, piercing through banana skin on one side. Lift out banana, being careful not to disturb skin; it will serve as a gondola-shaped container.

2. Slice each banana into small pieces. In a small bowl combine sliced bananas, chocolate chips, and marshmallows, and mix. Carefully spoon one quarter of mixture back into each banana skin.

3. Wrap stuffed banana skins in heavy-duty aluminum foil, sealing each packet well so skins won't leak.

4. Bury stuffed banana skins in coals producing low heat. Cook until marshmallows and chocolate melt and the banana is warm (about 15 minutes). Use caution when removing packets from coals as they may be quite hot. Remove foil and eat banana mixture with a spoon.

Serves 4.

BETTY'S PEAR TORTE

This torte comes out thin and crispy. You start making this dessert at home and finish it up in camp.

    2 tablespoons flour
    1 teaspoon baking powder
    ¼ teaspoon salt
    ¾ cup sugar
    ½ cup coarsely chopped walnuts
    2 canned pears, cut in
        1-inch chunks
    1 teaspoon vanilla extract
    1 egg
    2 teaspoons (approximately)
        butter, for preparing pan
    1½ cups cream or milk,
        for topping

At home:

Sift together flour, baking powder, and salt. Put into sealable plastic bag. Place sugar into another plastic bag; put walnuts into yet another. In a gallon-sized sealable plastic bag, put a can of pears, a bottle of vanilla, and the plastic bags with dry ingredients. Put a label on it with instructions on how to cook torte in camp. Make sure the perishables go in the cooler.

In camp:

1. Beat egg with a fork until light; add sugar and beat again, about 100 more strokes. Add flour mixture and stir, then stir in pears, nuts, and vanilla until just blended.

2. Smear butter all over the inside of a 10-inch nonstick skillet. Pour batter into skillet and cover the top with aluminum foil. Crumble a smaller piece of foil so it is wrinkled, put it over the foil lid, then put another layer of foil over that. The wrinkled foil creates air space above the lid, and that will protect your torte from being burned on the top when you cook it.

3. Bury pan in the campfire coals left over from cooking dinner. Bake for 30 minutes. To serve, remove pan from coals, cut torte into 6 pieces, put each on a plate, and pour a little cream on top.

Serves 6.

CAMPER'S COFFEE

You add the coffee grounds directly to the water in this version of hobo or cowboy coffee. Although no one seems to know why, when campers use the grounds again, it's called Eskimo coffee. Be sure to bring along milk or a powdered substitute and sugar or a substitute so all your camping companions can have their morning and evening coffee fix just the way they like it.

    10 cups water
    1½ cups regular-grind coffee

In camp:

1. In your camping coffeepot bring water to a boil. Stir in coffee and remove from heat. Cover pot and let steep for 5 to 10 minutes.

2. To serve, sprinkle about a ½ cup cold water in the pot to settle the grounds. Pour through a strainer into cups. Serve hot either black or with milk and sugar or honey.

Makes 10 cups strong coffee.

Mexican Mocha To prepare this after-dinner treat, mix equal parts Camper's Coffee with Mexican Hot Chocolate (see page 120) in a large mug. Top with whipped cream and sprinkle with powdered chocolate.

Irish Coffee For those who indulge, this San Francisco tradition makes quite a hit when served in the wilderness. To make, preheat coffee mugs with hot water. Drain. Pour in one jigger of Irish whiskey in each mug. Add ½ teaspoon of sugar and stir to dissolve. Pour in coffee. Top with at least ½ inch of whipped cream. Serve immediately.

WILDERNESS BRUNCH

*Fresh Papaya Halves
With Fresh Lime Squeeze*

Grilled Sage Sausage

Hash Brown Potatoes

Steamed Corn Bread

Dutch Oven Cowboy Eggs

*Beverage Suggestions: Tangerine
Juice, Mexican Hot Chocolate, and
Camper's Coffee (see page 117)*

---

*The pungent aroma of coffee
and wood smoke in the air,
the morning sun slanting
through the trees, and fine
food cooking on the camp-
fire—what better way to
start a summer day? This
hearty meal is a
combination of American
and Mexican elements. As it
takes a while to get the
campfire hot and to cook this
entire menu, serve a first
course of papaya halves with
a squeeze of fresh lime and
fresh or frozen tangerine
juice. There is a lot to eat;
serve this special meal in the
late morning and skip
lunch. Recipes serve 6 to 8.*

PREPARATION PLAN

Preparation time for this meal is
2 hours from when you start the
campfire. Once the fire is burning
well and you've assembled all ingredients and cooking equipment,
prepare the steaming pot for the corn
bread and start water for the coffee.
Prepare the coffee and hot chocolate.
When hungry campers smell the food
cooking, serve the first course. Make
the hash browns, which can stay
warm over a low-heat area of the
fire, and then heat the sauce for the
eggs. Cook the sausage and eggs last,
when the bread is nearly done.

GRILLED SAGE SAUSAGE

These easy and delicious sausage
patties can be spiced to the likes of
your group.

- 2 pounds lean ground pork
- ½ teaspoon salt
- 1 teaspoon pepper
- 1 tablespoon crushed sage
- ⅛ to ¼ teaspoon cayenne pepper (optional)
  Oil, for grill

At home:
In a large mixing bowl, combine all
ingredients except oil, taking care to
mix thoroughly. Shape mixture into
small patties about 4 inches across.
Wrap patties in waxed paper.

In camp:
When fire is ready, place patties on
oiled grill 4 to 6 inches above hot
coals. As an alternative, place patties
inside a long-handled, hinged wire
basket. Sausage is done when it looks
like a well-done hamburger (about 5
minutes per side).

Serves 6 to 8.

HASH BROWN POTATOES

Bake the potatoes at home or in the
coals the night before.

- 2 to 4 tablespoons butter
- 2 small onions, sliced in rings
- 4 to 6 potatoes, baked, sliced lengthwise, and cut in ¼-inch chunks
  Salt and pepper, to taste
- ⅓ cup chopped parsley

In camp:
When fire is ready, melt butter in
skillet and sauté onion rings. Add
potatoes and cook over coals that are
producing medium-high heat until
brown and crusty (about 15 minutes).
Season with salt and pepper. Stir in
chopped parsley before serving.

Serves 6 to 8.

STEAMED CORN BREAD

You won't get a brown, crisp crust
with the steaming method, but
you're not liable to burn this bread,
either. This is a moist, tender corn
bread with a texture almost like
pound cake. You can substitute dehydrated eggs and milk, if desired.

- 1 cup white cornmeal
- 1 cup flour
  Scant ¼ cup sugar
- 1 tablespoon baking powder
- ½ teaspoon salt
- ⅓ cup plus 1 tablespoon butter
- 1 egg, beaten
- 1 cup buttermilk

At home:
Sift together cornmeal, flour,
sugar, baking powder, and salt. Put in
a sealable plastic bag.

In camp:
1. When fire is ready, using a 3-quart
pot, melt butter. In another 3-quart
pot, combine egg and buttermilk.
Twirl butter to coat pot, then add
melted butter to egg mixture. Do not
wash first pot. Add dry ingredients to
egg mixture and stir until just
blended. Pour into the well-buttered
pot, and cover with a tight-fitting lid.

2. Place 3-quart pot inside a large
pot and prepare the pans for steaming (see page 109). Take care that
the steaming water doesn't come
above the lip of the 3-quart pot.

3. Make sure steaming water stays at
a constant boil and that it does not
boil away. The corn bread is cooked
when it pulls away a bit from the
sides of the pot and comes back into
shape after being pressed lightly
with a touch of the finger (about
45 minutes). Serve cut into wedges.

Makes 12 wedges.

Make brunch to please everyone on your camping trip. Early risers can exercise before eating; cooking aromas will get late sleepers up to enjoy the day.

DUTCH OVEN COWBOY EGGS

A piquant ranchero sauce sets off these custardy, slowly scrambled eggs.

- 1 onion, diced
- 1 large clove garlic, minced
- 2 fresh green chiles, seeds removed, sliced in rounds
- 2 to 3 fresh jalapeño chiles, seeds removed, sliced in rounds
- 1 teaspoon cumin seed, crushed
- ½ teaspoon dried oregano
- 2 tablespoons olive oil
- 2 cans (16 oz each) whole tomatoes with juice
- 1 can (12 oz) whole green chiles
- 2 teaspoons white vinegar
- 1 teaspoon sugar
- 4 small plum tomatoes, diced
- ⅓ to ½ cup chopped cilantro, plus cilantro for garnish
- 2 tablespoons butter
- 12 eggs, beaten
- ½ cup grated Monterey jack cheese
- 1 avocado, sliced, for garnish

At home:

1. In a medium skillet on the stove, sauté onion, garlic, green and jalapeño chiles, cumin, and oregano in olive oil for about 7 minutes.

2. Put canned tomatoes and canned chiles in food processor or blender and process just until there are small discernible chunks of vegetables. Add to sautéed mixture. Add vinegar and sugar and cook for 15 minutes at medium-low heat. Add plum tomatoes and cook 5 to 10 more minutes. Stir in chopped cilantro and remove from heat. Cool and pack in plastic container; makes 3 cups of sauce.

In camp:

1. Prepare campfire. Melt butter in Dutch oven; add eggs and cook over very gentle heat, stirring constantly, until eggs slowly thicken as a mass into a custard (about 15 minutes). While eggs cook, place sauce in a 3-quart pot to warm.

2. To serve, let diners top eggs with sauce to taste and add cheese, avocado, and cilantro garnish.

Serves 6 to 8.

Plan to serve Mexican Hot Chocolate as a warming brunch beverage for children and others on your camping trip who don't drink coffee. Bring along enough ingredients to serve it in the evening as well. For dessert around the campfire, pair hot chocolate with Baked Apples (see page 113) or Marshmallow Roast (see page 23), or mix with Camper's Coffee (see page 117) for a Mexican Mocha.

MEXICAN HOT CHOCOLATE

Some American grocery stores sell Mexican chocolate. If you can't get the original, this recipe tells how to create a good American substitute.

- 12 ounces unsweetened chocolate
- 1 teaspoon ground cinnamon
- 3 tablespoons sugar
- 8 cups milk

In camp:

1. In a 3-quart pot over coals, bring chocolate, cinnamon, sugar, and milk to a boil, stirring constantly. Remove from heat and let bubbling subside.

2. Return to heat and bring to a boil again. Remove from heat and beat with a wire whisk, spoon, or a fork until frothy.

Serves 8.

Special Note

...ON SOURCES AND SUPPLIES

The companies and organizations listed here are just a few of the many sources of specialty meats, sausage making equipment, outdoor cooking equipment, and camping information available in the United States.

In the case of manufacturers and suppliers of cooking and camping equipment, no attempt has been made to distinguish between those companies that publish mail-order catalogs and those that merely supply interested parties with names of local retailers who distribute their product.

In the case of the national parks, contact the regional office nearest the destination you are interested in to request a guide book to all parks and monuments in that area. Campground reservations must be made through individual parks.

Manufacturers, suppliers, and organizations interested in being listed on this page in future editions of this book should write to the publisher's office at the address listed on page 2.

Specialty Meats

Aidells Sausage Company
618 Coventry Road
Kensington, CA 94707
415 863-7485

Balducci's
334 East 11th Street
New York, NY 10003-7426
800 822-1444

Jugtown Mountain Smokehouse
P.O. Box 366
Flemington, NJ 08822
201 782-2421

New Braunfels Smokehouse
P.O. Box 1159
New Braunfels, TX 78131
512 625-7316

Fred Unsinger, Inc.
1030 N. Third Street
Milwaukee, WI 53203
414 276-9100

Sausage Casings and Equipment

Carlson Butcher Supply
50 Mendell #12
San Francisco, CA 94124
415 648-2601

The Sausage Maker
177 Military Road
Buffalo, NY 14702
716 876-5521

Grilling and Smoking Equipment

Cook 'n Cajun Water Smokers
P.O. Box 3726
Shreveport, LA 71103

MECO Water Smokers
800 251-7558

Weber-Stephen Products Company
200 East Daniels Road
Palatine, IL 60067

Williams-Sonoma
P.O. Box 7456
San Francisco, CA 94120
415 421-4242

Camping Equipment

Blackadar Boating
P.O. Box 1170
Salmon, ID 83467
800 545-3337

L. L. Bean
4321 Main Street
Freeport, ME 04033
800 221-4221

Camp Kitchen
P.O Box 296
La Mirada, CA 90637
714 739-5329

The Coleman Company, Inc.
P.O. Box 1762
Wichita, KS 67201

Nalgene Trail Products
P.O. Box 365
Rochester, NY 14602

The North Face
(stores in 18 locations)
Main office:
999 Harrison Street
Berkeley, CA 94710

Recreation Equipment, Inc.
P.O. Box 88125
Seattle, WA 98188
800 426-4840

Camping Information

Call of the Wild/
Outdoor Woman's School
2519 Cedar Street
Berkeley, CA 94708
415 849-9292

The Sierra Club
P.O. Box 7959
San Francisco, CA 94120

United States National Parks
Write or visit the regional office, listed below, that administers the area you are interested in visiting.

North Atlantic Region
15 State Street
Boston, MA 02109
Conn., Maine, Mass., N.H., N.J., N.Y., R.I., Vt.,

Mid-Atlantic Region
143 South Third Street
Philadelphia, PA 19106
Del., Md., Pa., Va., W.Va.

Southeast Region
Richard Russell Building
75 Spring Street, SW
Atlanta, GA 30303
Ala., Fla., Ga., Ky., Miss., N.C., S.C., Tenn., P.R., V.I.

Midwest Region
1709 Jackson Street
Omaha, NE 68102
Ind., Ill., Iowa, Kans., Mich., Minn., Mo., Nebr., Ohio, Wis.

Rocky Mountain Region
655 Parfet Street
P.O. Box 25287
Denver, CO 80225
Colo., Mont., N.D., Utah, Wyo.

Southwest Region
1100 Old Santa Fe Trail
P.O. Box 728
Santa Fe, NM 87501
Ark., La., N.M., Okla., Tex.

Western Region
450 Golden Gate Avenue
Box 36063
San Francisco, CA 94102
Calif., Hawaii, Nev., most of Ariz.

Pacific Northwest Region
83 South King Street
Suite 212
Seattle, WA 98104
Idaho, Ore., Wash.

Alaska Region
2525 Gaambell Street
Anchorage, AK 99503

INDEX

Special Thanks

From Jill Fox to
Linda Bouchard
Joseph Feuling
Paula Schlosser

From Ron Clark to
Ed Poole and Chuck Woodside of
Weber-Stephen Products Company
Pu Kirdpirote of S.F. Bar-B-Q
Bobby Fulghum of Parker's Barbeque
Chris Rishell
Mary Christensen
Dianne and Josie Platner
John King
Bruce Aidells

From Bruce Aidells to
Linda Gottschalk
Cynthia Scheer
Jay Harlow
Michael Goodwin
Naomi Wise
Lonnie Gandara

From Carole Latimer to
Hope McGrath
JoAnne Rogers
Anne Dowie
Judith Calson
Burr Snider
Bolfing's Elmwood Hardware
Lone Star Industries

From Ernie Friedlander to
Kathy Friedlander
Kirk Amyx
Erin Allison

From Joanne Dexter to
Don Dexter
Marian Sullivan
Sue White
Kim Dankmyer
Shelly Gillan
Pam Christionson

From Janet Nusbaum to
Debra Estrin
Vera and Arthur Nusbaum
Karletta Moniz
Lazzari Fuel Company
Swane Adeney
Williams-Sonoma
Mitchell Nusbaum
la Ville du Soleil
Made in U.S.A.
Shaun Weisbach
Tony Cowan
The Exclusive Cutlery Shop

U.S. MEASURE AND METRIC MEASURE
CONVERSION CHART

		Formulas for Exact Measures			**Rounded Measures for Quick Reference**		
	Symbol	When you know:	Multiply by:	To find:			
Mass (Weight)	oz	ounces	28.35	grams	1 oz		= 30 g
	lb	pounds	0.45	kilograms	4 oz		= 115 g
	g	grams	0.035	ounces	8 oz		= 225 g
	kg	kilograms	2.2	pounds	16 oz	= 1 lb	= 450 g
					32 oz	= 2 lb	= 900 g
					36 oz	= 2¼ lb	= 1000g (1 kg)
Volume	tsp	teaspoons	5.0	milliliters	¼ tsp	= ¹⁄₂₄ oz	= 1 ml
	tbsp	tablespoons	15.0	milliliters	½ tsp	= ¹⁄₁₂ oz	= 2 ml
	fl oz	fluid ounces	29.57	milliliters	1 tsp	= ⅙ oz	= 5 ml
	c	cups	0.24	liters	1 tbsp	= ½ oz	= 15 ml
	pt	pints	0.47	liters	1 c	= 8 oz	= 250 ml
	qt	quarts	0.95	liters	2 c (1 pt)	= 16 oz	= 500 ml
	gal	gallons	3.785	liters	4 c (1 qt)	= 32 oz	= 1 liter
	ml	milliliters	0.034	fluid ounces	4 qt (1 gal)	= 128 oz	= 3¾ liter
Length	in.	inches	2.54	centimeters	⅜ in.	= 1 cm	
	ft	feet	30.48	centimeters	1 in.	= 2.5 cm	
	yd	yards	0.9144	meters	2 in.	= 5 cm	
	mi	miles	1.609	kilometers	2½ in.	= 6.5 cm	
	km	kilometers	0.621	miles	12 in. (1 ft)	= 30 cm	
	m	meters	1.094	yards	1 yd	= 90 cm	
	cm	centimeters	0.39	inches	100 ft	= 30 m	
					1 mi	= 1.6 km	
Temperature	°F	Fahrenheit	⁵⁄₉ (after subtracting 32)	Celsius	32°F	= 0°C	
					68°F	= 20°C	
	°C	Celsius	⁹⁄₅ (then add 32)	Fahrenheit	212°F	= 100°C	
Area	in.²	square inches	6.452	square centimeters	1 in.²	= 6.5 cm²	
	ft²	square feet	929.0	square centimeters	1 ft²	= 930 cm²	
	yd²	square yards	8361.0	square centimeters	1 yd²	= 8360 cm²	
	a.	acres	0.4047	hectares	1 a.	= 4050 m²	